BOROBUDUR

BOROBUDUR

Jacques Dumarçay

Edited and translated by
MICHAEL SMITHIES

Singapore
OXFORD UNIVERSITY PRESS
Oxford New York

Oxford University Press

Oxford London New York Toronto
Kuala Lumpur Singapore Hong Kong Tokyo
Delhi Bombay Calcutta Madras Karachi
Nairobi Dar es Salaam Cape Town
Melbourne Auckland

and associates in
Beirut Berlin Ibadan Mexico City

OXFORD is a trademark of Oxford University Press

© *Oxford University Press 1978*
First published 1978
Fourth impression 1985

ISBN 0 19 580379 5

Printed in Malaysia by Peter Chong Printers Sdn. Bhd.
Published by Oxford University Press,
10, New Industrial Road, Singapore 1953.

Preface

BOROBUDUR draws a great number of sightseers. In 1974 the authorities recorded 260,000 paying visitors, including 31,650 foreign tourists; these figures take no account of the days when entry is free (17 August, the Indonesian National Day, and Lebaran, the holiday at the end of Ramadan) when there are such huge crowds that a one-way system has to be enforced on the stairways. It is best to avoid these days if the architectural details of the monument are to be appreciated fully. Most visitors come in April and October, when there are rather more than 2,500 a day, rising to 5,000 and more on Sundays.

The monument naturally means different things to different persons, and visitors come for any number of reasons, but the remark made by Sultan Hamengku Buwono IX of Yogyakarta, Vice-President of the Indonesian Republic, to the journalist, Terry Baudert, summarizes what many Indonesians generally feel about the monument: 'You must remember that it was built as a place of meditation, not of worship; that is important'.

The restoration work, and particularly the dismantling of the monument, gave me the chance to study the internal structure of Borobudur and to appreciate the history of architecture better. I have only given here a general survey which takes no account of the numerous changes, for example, in the doorways, inevitable over such a length of time. My work was only made possible by the constant support of Michael Smithies who showed himself a meticulous editor and translator and took a large part in the compilation of this text. My sincere thanks to him and to my wife, my observant first reader, and lastly to the Badan Pemugaran Candi Borobudur, which gave me permission to use its admirable resources.

Borobudur   JACQUES DUMARÇAY
January 1977

Contents

CRXXXC

Maps and Plans

Colour Plates

Black and White Plates

Introduction

HINDU-Javanese art was appreciated rather late by Europeans. In the eighteenth century, the gentlemen of the Dutch East Indies Company were preoccupied by commerce although, as Bosch noted, when they went to the court of Mataram the road they took passed right by the temple at Prambanan. This lack of interest was not particular to these merchants but was general for the whole of Europe. Such knowledge as there was of Indian art was deformed by a rather Islamic view of its statuary. In his *Histoire de la Révolution des Etats du Grand Mogol* which appeared in 1670, Bernier really only described what he saw and appreciated in Indo-Islamic art; the statues are mentioned only as religious objects. When in unusual cases a traveller expressed an opinion, like Rogerius, for example, describing what he saw on the Coromandel coast in 1672, it was to find the sculpture, with all those heads and arms, abominable. Even recently the sculptured forms of India and the states under Hindu influence still had to be explained, not always satisfactorily; Mus spoke of the multiplicity of arms and heads as a kind of static cinema and Stern describes the many heads as being a manifestation of the omnipresence of the divinity.

At the beginning of the eighteenth century, in spite of an increasing interest in the Orient (Chardin's *Travels* were published in 1711, those of Tavernier in 1719, Galland's *Thousand and One Nights* in 1717, the *Persian Letters* of Montesquieu in 1721 and were at once translated into several European languages), the art of India and Java was either despised or ignored. However, in 1756 Charles de Brosses published his *Histoire des Navigations aux Terres Australes* in which he discussed the interest of recent discoveries in a new manner and expressed the hope that explorers would not just look for places for commercial exploitation but also for glory and greater geographical knowledge. This book had some influence when, ten years later, Bougainville undertook his world tour. His was a proper scientific expedition complete with a naturalist and an astronomer. They landed at Batavia in September 1768 and stayed in Java until November. Unfortunately this *Voyage*, which was published from 1771 to 1773, did not have much influence as many readers thought it was scarcely conceivable that one could travel round the world and not go to China.

In 1778 the founder of the first masonic lodge in Batavia, Radermacher, established the 'Batavian Society for the Arts and the Sciences'. He took as his model the learned societies which sprang up in the wake of the influence of the *Encyclopédie* and the Enlightenment. At the beginning the work of the society was not concerned with research but with technical progress, taking little account of history or art. However, at this period there existed no similar association in East Asia. The transactions the society kept until the end of the nineteenth century bear the mark of their origins both in the masonic movement and the Encyclopédie. The study of Borobudur by Leemans which appeared in 1873 pays much attention to stone cutting and the quality of the masonry.

After a brief Napoleonic interlude, the British took over the administration of Java. In 1811 Thomas Stamford Raffles was created Lieutenant-Governor of Java by the Governor-General of India. It was Raffles who was the first to understand the importance of Borobudur. In 1814 he ordered Cornelius, a surveyor at Semarang, to inspect the monument. After visiting Borobudur on 18 May 1815, Raffles noted in his Journal:

In addition to their claim on the consideration of the antiquarian, the ruins of two of these places, Brambana and Boro Bodo, are admirable as majestic works of art, the great extent of the masses of buildings covered, in some parts, with the luxuriant vegetation of the climate, the beauty and delicate execution of the separate portions, the symmetry and regularity of the whole, the great number and interesting character of the statues and the bas-reliefs, with which they are ornamented, excite our wonder that they were not earlier examined, sketched and described.

Raffles, following the example of Marsden's *The History of Sumatra* (1811), wrote *The History of Java* which appeared in London in 1817.

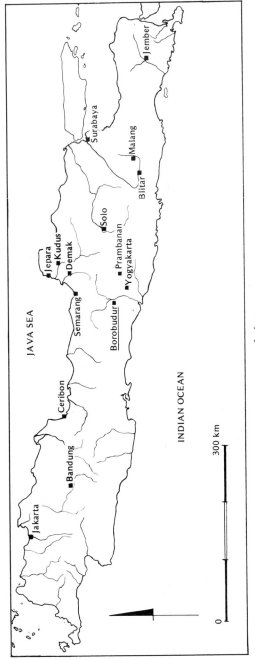

1. Java

This quite remarkable book, however, only mentions the antiquities briefly. But Borobudur is described in it for the first time and all the monuments are grouped as being of the same period, with Candi Sukuh on Mount Lawu correctly being considered as of a different period. Raffles' main collaborator, John Crawfurd, published in 1820 in Edinburgh his *History of the Indian Archipelago*. This book was taken up and enlarged in 1856 with the title of *A Descriptive Dictionary of the Indian Islands and Adjacent Countries*. Crawfurd was enthusiastic about the architecture he described, but disapproved of the sculpture. After this activity stimulated by Raffles, several years passed without anything new being written about the monumental art of Java.

However, knowledge about the Javanese monuments began to spread. The philosopher, Amiel, made allusion to them in his *Journal* in 1866 and finally the Batavian Society published the work of Leemans, who made much use of the drawings of Cornelius, supplemented with others by J. Wilsen and Schonberg Mulder. The book appeared in 1873 in Dutch and in French. At more or less the same time, in 1872, the Batavian Society commissioned a complete photographic survey of the monument. The photographer appointed, Kinsbergen, gave up the idea of covering it completely. He found that the monument was not completely cleared and complained that there were four feet of debris in some parts. For the first time in reports, mention is made of the subsidence of the first and third galleries. Kinsbergen, when he cleared the paving, also undertook the first restoration work. He filled the hollows in the paving with sand so that the rain-water would run out of the gargoyles, instead of staying in the gallery. Two of the prints of these first photographs were found by Segalen among the papers of Gauguin in Tahiti, and one of them, showing a relief on the first gallery, is probably the inspiration for the painting called 'Et l'or de leur corps' which can be seen in the Musée du Jeu de Paume in Paris.

The work of clearing the monument continued. This led to the discovery of the hidden reliefs by the Dutch archaeologist Brandes in 1886. These were excavated under the direction of Ijzerman in 1890. After these discoveries interest in the monument grew and the decision to restore Borobudur was made. The work was carried out from 1907 to 1911 under Van Erp. The means at his disposal were very limited so he could not undertake even a partial dismantling of the monument. He tried to stabilize the walls by getting rid of the rain-water permeating the foundations. He used the same method for this as Kinsbergen but instead of filling the hollows with sand he used concrete of very varied quality. This was covered over with a paving of andesite which allowed the water to flow out of the original gargoyles. When concrete was not necessary, the joints in the original paving were opened and filled with mortar.

The circular terraces were entirely relaid with new material on the ruins of the old and the pierced stupas were completely reconstructed, some with new stones. After this work, Borobudur regained something of its original appearance. It was not until 1931 that a law was enacted protecting historic monuments in Indonesia. Archaeological research continued and mention is made in this text of some of the more important contributions.

Van Erp's restoration work was shown to be insufficient. The monument continued to shift and different parts were dismantled to avoid collapse, especially the balustrades on the north side. Soekmono launched in 1968 the 'Save Borobudur' appeal which was taken up by the Indonesian government and UNESCO. They ordered numerous studies of the climatic conditions, local earthquakes, the settlement which had occurred since 1914, the structure of the surrounding soils, local petrography, biology and botany in relation to the monument. The conclusion of these studies was that the damage caused to Borobudur came essentially from the rain-water and the existence of a large amount of water in the hill which escapes through the joints in the vertical stone walls and leaves particles of soil on the surface of the reliefs. The humidity leads to a growth of algae, mosses, lichens, fungi and bacteria. The general recommendations behind the project are, firstly, to eliminate the water coming from the hill by installing a suitable drainage system, secondly, to clean the bas-reliefs and remove all the growths on the surface of the stone and, thirdly, to re-erect the monument.

The project was prepared on the civil engineering side by a Dutch firm and United Nations experts and personnel supplied by several countries under bilateral aid programmes to Indonesia advised on the treatment of the stone and the problems involved in the restoration. The project can be divided into three main phases: dismantling, treat-

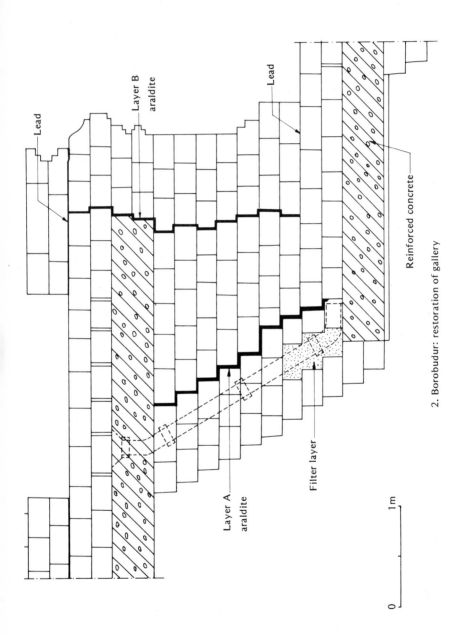

Lead

Layer B
araldite

Lead

Reinforced concrete

Layer A
araldite

Filter layer

2. Borobudur: restoration of gallery

0   1 m

ment of the stone and reconstruction. It was considered that the upper terraces which had been restored by Van Erp were in sufficiently good condition and did not have to be dismantled. The base, being well preserved, was in no need of restoration either. The work is therefore limited to the galleries containing the bas-reliefs. The dismantling by itself is relatively simple but given the large number of stones—more than 1,600,000—the numbering has to be done very carefully and under close supervision; the difficulty of finding a wrongly numbered stone can easily be imagined.

The monument is mainly constructed with andesite, a stone of volcanic origin. However, it is not the classic type and is closer to augite-andesite which can be found all around the Pacific. This stone has a porosity that varies greatly from 11 to 46 per cent. The highly porous nature of the stone encourages vegetal growths. The mosses are very difficult to eliminate, since the atmospheric humidity is sufficient to sustain their growth. The ferns can survive on very little earth but can probably be entirely eliminated. The lichens form by far the most widespread growths and are difficult to destroy because, like the mosses, they can live off the humidity in the atmosphere. They cause the greatest damage to the structure, apart from the unlovely appearance they give to the stone. Some lichens are acidic and in contact with rain-water can cause the stones underneath them to be eroded. The roots of the lichens also penetrate the pores of the stone and cause them to split. Finally the algae are often found together with the mosses and in these cases hasten the corrosion of the stone; they develop above all in the water coming from the hill underneath the monument.

Depending on whether a stone is merely exposed to rain-water or additionally to water coming from the hill, it can be the host to different growths and consequently suffer different kinds of damage. This can be seen in the monument where the changes in the balustrades are not the same as those in the retaining walls which are in contact with the hill. It was decided therefore to eliminate as much as possible, if not all, the water seeping out of the hill. To do this, the restoration project involves the provision of two successive shields of araldite, a tar epoxy adhesive. Water will be retained behind the walls, collected on concrete slabs, and led away by a drainage system to the edges of the hill. The stones broken by the lichens have to be put together again. It is possible that the protective shields will not eliminate the growths for which the atmospheric humidity is sufficient to survive; consequently some of the lichens and mosses will reappear especially where the stone has itself as high a porosity as 46 per cent.

The main interest of the project is not in the treatment of the stone but in the mechanical aspect of the dismantling of the monument and the means used to reconstruct it. Borobudur (as will be seen in Chapter 4) is constructed on a natural hill, enlarged by fill which supports the stone structure. The abundant rainfall of central Java (2 074 mm or 81.65 inches at Borobudur in 1970), gets through to the fill and carries away fine particles of it as it seeps out. This causes the noticeable shifting of the monument which can be as much as 10°. The extraordinary cohesion of the masonry has stood up to these movements but the settlement of the monument has been considerable, by as much as 80 cm.

Van Erp did not try to correct these effects, particularly on the circular terraces, the ruins of which were disguised by rebuilding with new stones, sometimes very freely. As moreover the base is not being touched, the calculation of the new measurements has to be made within these limits, that is, between the base and the first circular terrace; this is in spite of re-erecting the walls of the balustrades and the bas-reliefs. Several adjustments to the levels are therefore necessary so that the first circular terrace is not obliterated.

The re-erection of the structure is carried out on reinforced concrete slabs about 5 m wide which completely surround the monument at 45 cm below the level of the reconstructed paving and under each of the galleries and balustrade walls. These four cement rings will give a new cohesion to the monument, for the settlement and the dismantling have reduced the holding quality of the original structure. This explains the need for considerable stability in the concrete slabs which are 60 cm thick and which have to stand up to seismic jolts as well as the normal stresses and strains caused by the building; Borobudur is located in a zone where there is a fair amount of earthquake activity, between points VI and VII on the Rossi-Forel scale.[1]

To prevent continual removal from the fill by the permeating water causing a constant sinking, a layer of sand, the grain size of which decreases from the top to the bottom, has been laid to hold back the earth from the fill while still allowing the water to flow away.

In sum the internal stability of the monument now rests on five slabs of reinforced concrete corresponding to each of the galleries and the upper level supporting the circular terraces. On these slabs the walls containing the bas-reliefs and the balustrades are reconstructed; internally they are protected by two screens of araldite and at the base by a lead sheet to prevent upward capillary action. This is completed by a filter which keeps back the particles of the fill and stops them being carried off by the water permeating through the monument. All this work, even though aided by modern equipment, is expected to take several years to complete, for the size of the restoration operation is considerable.

[1] VI. Fairly strong shock. General awakening of those asleep; general ringing of church bells; oscillation of chandeliers; stopping of clocks; visible agitation of trees and shrubs; some startled persons leaving their dwellings.

VII. Strong shock. Overthrow of movable objects; fall of plaster; ringing of church bells; general panic, without damage to buildings.

1

The Historical Setting

THE two main historical sources for the states of the Hindu period in the Indonesian archipelago are the inscriptions left by the rulers and dignitaries of the kingdoms and Chinese chronicles. These sources give very limited information; the inscriptions mostly describe religious foundations and the Chinese chronicles are principally concerned with embassies sent to the imperial court.

THE HINDU PERIOD

The Hindu period in the states in the archipelago, and more generally in southern Asia, was not brought about by force. There was no conquest or colonization as with the European countries in the nineteenth century. Van Leur has shown that Hinduism was not established in the wake of commerce. The Hindu penetration was brought about by cultural and especially religious circumstances, by the use of Sanskrit for inscriptions and the adoption of a complete and coherent Hindu or Buddhist mythology. This is hardly the domain of traders. At the time when it is generally agreed that the Hindu period was beginning in the area, in the first centuries of the Christian era, it is likely that Sanskrit in India was already not a truly living language but restricted to religious affairs.

The Hindu period was most likely brought about by the influence of priests who depended on small kingdoms which existed before they arrived and which were inextricably associated with the proper working of the irrigation systems and a religion which allowed for the deification of rulers' origins. The great success of Mahayana Buddhism, as will be seen later, was assured since it permitted the assimilation of the king to a Bodhisattva (a future Buddha) and so reinforced the temporal authority of the ruler. It would seem therefore that for a large part Hindu influence was due to the initiative of princes in the archipelago who attracted Brahmins and perhaps artisans to their courts. Although Chinese influence is not as strong as Indian, it is technically discernible in the wooden buildings and also in the use of tiles.

The first Hindu institution in Java of which record has come down to us is mentioned in the Sanskrit inscriptions of about A.D. 450 from the south of Jakarta. Their author was Purnavarman, a king of Taruma, and one of these inscriptions mentions the opening of a canal.

SAILENDRA AND SANJAYA

In Java, between the inscriptions of Purnavarman in the fifth century and the Cangal inscription of 732 on Gunung Wukir near Borobudur, records are sketchy and uninteresting and their interpretation allows for innumerable hypotheses. The author of the Cangal text, King Sanjaya, is probably a Mataram prince but about whom little is known. His successor, King Panongkaran, is cited in the Kalasan inscription of 778. Van Naerssen has shown that this king, who ordered the construction of Kalasan, was only a tributary king to the Sailendra dynasty. This may also be the case for Sanjaya. In 1950, de Casparis examined all the information in the Sailendra dynasty inscriptions. He concluded that during the period from the end of the eighth century to the beginning of the ninth century two dynasties shared power in central Java. He established the succession in the following way:

Sanjaya	Sailendra
Sanjaya 732–±760	Bhanu 752–?
Panongkaran ±760–778–±780	Visnu (Dharmatunga)?–775–782
Panunggalan ±780–±800	Indra (Sangramadhanomjaya)
Warak ±800–before 819 or 829	782–812–before 824
Garung (= Patapan?) 819–829–842	Samaratunga 824–832
Pikatan 842–850–856	
Kayuwani 856–863–882	

The dates in italics are confirmed by an inscription; the others were established by de Casparis.

For the dates of Indra and Samaratunga in the Sailendra dynasty Damais proposed the following correction: for Indra 784–792 and for Samaratunga 792 to about 833. After this date, de Casparis thinks that the Sanjaya became completely independent of the Sailendra. The appearance of the latter in Java is an event of great importance for the origin of Borobudur since it is this dynasty which established Mahayana Buddhism and caused the Hindu worshippers who had constructed the Dieng temples to move eastward. This eastward movement is confirmed by a Sanskrit inscription dating from 760 discovered in the Malang region and mentioning the construction of a temple dedicated to Agastya. The Chinese chronicles also tell of the displacement of the capital to the east. During this relatively short period from 760 to 800, the Sailendra dynasty probably established suzerainty over Cambodia and tried several times, in 767, 774, and 787, to establish themselves without much success on the east coast of Indo-China. About 800, in the reign of Indra, the power of the dynasty experienced a certain decline and it was at this point, in 802, that the Khmer prince Jayavarman II definitively freed himself of all subservience to Java.

Coedès thought that towards 820 the Hindus who had emigrated to the east regained power by reuniting central and east Java. This would be connected with the Sanjaya dynasty which was completely freed of the suzerainty of the Sailendra in 832–833. This Hindu renaissance showed itself in the construction of the whole ensemble of Prambanan, the consecration date of which is 856. In spite of this return of Hinduism, which must have been accompanied by a new cultural wave from India, Buddhism continued to flourish. The reigning princes founded several new temples and made gifts to Buddhist sanctuaries. In 860 and 873 the Chinese emperor sent embassies to Java. An echo of this visit can be found in the *New History of the T'ang* which says that the Javanese 'make fortifications of wood, and even the big houses are covered in palm thatch. They have ivory beds and matting made of the bark of bamboo. The country produces tortoise-shell, gold, silver, rhinoceros horns and ivory.... They have an alphabet and have a knowledge of astronomy.'

THE BUILDERS OF BOROBUDUR

It is very difficult, from this chronological schema, to decide which princes ordered the construction of the different stages of Borobudur. However, there is a technical indication, as will be seen later, which allows the fifth period of construction to be dated approximately. The process in question was only used after the building of Prambanan. The fifth period of construction can readily be seen as the taking over of Borobudur by the Sanjaya, freed of Sailendra control, about 833.

The previous stages are the work of the Sailendras. The Buddhist temple of Kalasan was certainly constructed by a Sanjaya but one who confirms his dependence on the Sailendras. The founding of a temple became a political rather than a religious act; the vassal constructed a temple for the gods of his suzerain. The initiative for the first period of Borobudur appears to be contemporary with the reign of Visnu, about 780. The second and third periods of construction of Borobudur and the second Mendut can be attributed to his successor Indra. The last two periods show a profound change in conception, not only architectural but also, it would seem, doctrinal. This movement is general and can be seen in the important changes in Candi Sewu probably marked by the inscription of 792, the first known text in Old Malay found in Java. The fourth period, of no great importance, already marks a decline in the dynasty and is probably the work of Samaratunga who is named in the inscription of 824 discovered at Karangtenah. Whatever interpretation one puts on this text, neither the sovereign is in question nor the fact that it concerns an endowment made to Buddhist temples, among which Borobudur can be counted, even if it is not mentioned for certain.

In sum, the approximate dates in the construction of Borobudur can be fixed as follows:

±780   The pegging out of the first monument and the first period of construction

±792   Second and third periods of construction, and the complete reconstruction of the monument

±824   Fourth period

±833   Fifth period

After this last date, the monument continued to be used until the tenth century; T'ang period potteries have been found on the site.

Some activity doubtless continued to the fourteenth century at least and the monument is probably indicated in the *Negarakertagama*, a Javanese text of the middle of the fourteenth century. Its author greatly admired the Vajradhara Buddhist sect and lists the main sanctuaries where the sect practised its rites at the time he was writing. Among them is one called Budur, which is most probably Borobudur (Canto 77, Stanza 3).

2

The Religious Setting

THERE is little documentary evidence to consult when attempting to determine the religious environment at the time of the building of Borobudur. There are some inscriptions, the statues and reliefs of Borobudur itself and other contemporary monuments, and a few subsequent texts which can be linked to its architectural symbolism, in particular the *Sang Hyang Kamahayanikan*, a Sanskrit catechism which is linked with a text in Old Javanese. Using these sources, Krom concluded that the religious milieu in which Borobudur was created was Buddhist of the Mahayanist school. The belief in the five Jinas (the Dhyani Buddhas) was general and a special cult was attached to the Bodhisattvas and to the Goddess Tara.

Buddhism is a doctrine of salvation which in some essential elements stems from Hinduism. The doctrine was preached for the first time by the Buddha whose name was Siddartha Gautama and who belonged to the Sakya clan, whence the name Sakyamuni (the sage of the Sakya clan) by which he was often known. He was born about 566 B.C. at Lumbini, near Kapilavastu, at the foot of the Himalayas in a small state ruled by his father. When Siddartha was sixteen years old, he married and had a son. The soothsayers at the time of his birth had indicated that he would not become king if he saw an old, sick or dead person and every effort was made to prevent him seeing them. However, in 537 B.C. revelation came to him through encounters with age, sickness and death. He was revolted by the world, left his family and became a wandering mystic. He first of all practised Yoga but doubted the validity of the method for, having achieved what should have been a state of ecstasy, he found himself the same as before. He then gave himself over to asceticism but seeing that he achieved nothing by it he gave up and went to Bodh Gaya. There, under a tree, he sat down to meditate, directing his thoughts to the mystery of death and rebirth; during the night he became enlightened. He continued his meditation for some time and then went to Benares where he preached a sermon which contained the essence of the Buddhist doctrine.

See, brothers, the holy truth about pain; birth is pain, age is pain, sickness is pain, death is pain; union with those one does not like is pain, separation from those one loves is pain, not to succeed in one's aim is pain; the five forms of attachment are pain. See, brothers, the holy truth about the origin of pain; it is desire which leads from one reincarnation to another, accompanied by pleasure and envy, which now and again is satisfied; the desire for pleasure, the desire for the material, and desire for the impermanent. See, brothers, the holy truth of the suppression of pain; the extinction of this desire by the complete destruction of desire. Desire is banished and forsaken; one is liberated from it and it has no further place. (After Foucher.)

The cycle of rebirths (samsara) has its origin in eternity; it is impossible to discover its beginning. Rebirth according to Buddhist tradition follows five possible destinies, hell, animals, spirits, men and gods, in three different worlds. Firstly comes the world of desire, where the five senses comprise most destinies, those of hell, animals, spirits, men and some of the gods. Then there is the world of subtle nature or of pure form which comprises celestial beings reborn in the world of Brahma and scattered through the spheres of the four ecstasies (dyana). Finally, there is the immaterial world or, beyond the world of form, the world of beings reborn in the spheres of the four meditations; the place where space is infinite, where knowledge is infinite, the place of nothingness and ultimately where there is neither consciousness nor unconsciousness.

The preaching and practice of Buddha lasted forty years; he travelled all through the valley of the Ganges, returned several times to Kapilavastu where he converted his father, wife and son, and founded a monastic community but never became its head. Buddha effaced himself before the law he had discovered and only considered himself its servant and in no way divine. Sakyamuni shows the path and cannot help those who cannot follow it.

In 486 B.C. Buddha fell ill and predicted his imminent death. He ate a dish of pork and caught dysentery; he went to Kusinagara and rose to Nirvana. His body was burnt, and the remains were scattered in ten directions: eight consisted of ashes, the ninth consisted of the urn and the tenth, the cinders of the fire. Over each of these parts, which were carried away by believers, a stupa was erected.

Nirvana presents a double aspect. It is first of all the suppression of all desire and then the end of pain and of all existence. This moral perfection cannot be attained in one terrestrial life and many previous lives have to be lived through. The gesture so often shown of taking the earth as witness (the right hand pointing down to the earth) symbolizes the long preparation necessary and which has the earth as witness at each rebirth. This perfection is expressed not only morally but also by an invisible and glorified body for the contemporaries of Sakyamuni. When the sculptors sought a physical portrayal of the Buddha, they did not try to find a likeness to the historical person but showed his glorified body based on the lists of marks by which one recognizes the Buddha. These lists have reference to a young child because that is what the astrologers had in mind; this explains the curious proportions of some statues.

Soon after Buddhism's initial successes, there was a movement to elaborate the doctrine. About 100 B.C. a text, the *Prajnaparamita*, which can be translated as 'Transcendental Wisdom', was compiled. It forms the kernel of the new doctrine, Mahayana or the Greater Vehicle. Its followers derisively called the old school Hinayana, or Lesser Vehicle.

Mahayana originated for the most part in a sect whose doctrinal texts have been almost entirely destroyed, the *Mahasanghika*, which developed in the Magada in the north of India and also around Amaravati in southern India. According to Conze, the two key words of Mahayana are 'Bodhisattva' and 'void'. The Bodhisattva is a being who wants to become a Buddha. In this way Siddartha before his illumination was a Bodhisattva. The big difference between the saints of the Lesser Vehicle and the future Buddhas of the Greater Vehicle is that the latter do not only seek to attain Nirvana for themselves, but also want to be instrumental in helping others to escape from pain. This concept led to the identification of the sovereign with a Bodhisattva assuring the well-being of his kingdom. However the ideal of future

Buddhas is not only compassion; they still have to see, in their infinite wisdom, that all things are empty. Buddhism is not troubled by this contradiction: the Bodhisattva wishes to save beings who are only outward forms. The contradiction is clearly established, but an explanation is not attempted. In the Buddhist void, which is the only ultimate reality, there is no duality; the object does not differ from the subject, nor does Nirvana differ from the world, nor does being differ from non-being.

The Greater, like the Lesser, Vehicle only envisages salvation at some remote future time. Even if Mahayana shortens this period of time, the number of rebirths before reaching Nirvana is still considerable. So there is recourse to magic, rituals, formulae, gymnastics, and breath control to speed the path to Buddhahood. These techniques, which are not only Buddhist, form the Tantra and are divided into two groups: the Tantra of the right hand, which puts into value the masculine principle of creative energy, and that of the left hand, which emphasizes above all the female principles. In Buddhism, the Tantra of the left hand constitutes the Vajrayana school which began about the year A.D. 300 in the north of India.

Tantric Buddhism stresses an important mythology which rests on the five Jinas (which are also called the Dhyani Buddhas): Vairocana, the illuminated or the brilliant one, Aksobhya, the imperturbable one, Ratnasambhava, issued from a jewel, Amithaba, infinite light, and Amoghasida, eternal success. These five Buddhas are not ordinary Buddhas who have reached their state through numerous rebirths; they are Buddhas of all eternity, having never been anything else, and comprise the body of the universe. Each one is mirrored in a celestial Bodhisattva and in a terrestrial Buddha and rules over a whole family of lesser celestial beings.

Early Buddhism was strictly masculine, and the female sex was an obstacle to supreme realization. So when the disciple Ananda asked the Buddha, 'How should we behave to women?', the master replied, 'Do not see them.' 'But what if we should see them?' 'Do not speak to them.' 'And if we have to speak to them?' 'Control your thoughts.' But with Tantrism a cult of female divinities spread, especially of Prajnaparamita, which is not only a text but a goddess, and Tara, who aids the believer to cross obstacles separating him from salvation.

The main rites practised by Buddhists are centred on the monastic community which is given alms. The monk must receive any gift, from the humblest to the most magnificent, in the same way. One of the Buddhist saints did not reject a finger which had fallen off a leper into his begging bowl. In principle, each monastery in addition to the necessary buildings for the material life of the community, such as cells, a dining hall, and a meeting room, includes a sanctuary containing statues, but the most characteristic monument of Buddhism to be found in a monastery is the stupa. Initially this was doubtless conceived as a reliquary; the placing of relics symbolically gives life to a monument. Gradually, the stupa came to be a major symbol in itself. One of the essential rites of the Buddhist community is linked to the stupa, and this is the *pradakshina* which consists in moving around the structure keeping it always on the right hand. Another pious obligation for the believer is the beautification and enrichment of the sanctuary. This was principally accomplished by Javanese Buddhists by means of numerous inscriptions, in particular at Candi Plaosan. These preserve the memory of foundations created by the senior officials of the kingdom who had small sanctuaries built around those of the reigning prince near the principal sanctuary.

Buddhism appeared in the archipelago in all probability in the early centuries of the Christian era: a bronze Buddha recalling the Amaravati styles of the fourth to the fifth century was found at Sempaga in Sulawesi (Celebes). There was no apparent transition between a neolithic civilization and conversion to Buddhism. Another statue of the Buddha, being closer to those from Ceylon of the fourth to the sixth century, was discovered at Jember in east Java. This and other evidence is too fragmentary for any deduction as to the form of Buddhism practised at the time. However, it was probably the Lesser Vehicle, for in the middle of the seventh century, a Chinese pilgrim, Houi Ning, settled in Java and translated into Chinese the Hinayanist Sanskrit texts. Mahayana appeared in the Malay peninsula where inscriptions of the fifth or sixth century carried Mahayanist lines. The expansion of the Greater Vehicle into the islands took place at the beginning of the eighth century under the influence of the University of Nalanda in Bengal, and it was supported by the Pala dynasty which was then reigning there. This source is not the only one. One can find Singalese influence in an inscription discovered at Ratu Baka, near Prambanan, dated 792, shortly after the Kalasan inscription of 778. Mention is made in this text of a monastery called Abhayagiri Vihara very similar to the name of the famous monastery of Anuradhapura, the old capital of Ceylon. The form of Buddhism mentioned in the Ratu Baka inscription is Mahayanist. De Casparis translated it and thought that monks were banished from their monastery because of Mahayanist doctrinal deviation at the time of the Hinayanist re-establishment in Anuradhapura, and that they are directly the cause of the Abhayagiri Vihara in Java. Nevertheless, de Casparis notes that the Singalese chronicles do not mention the expulsion of monks in the second half of the eighth century. Mahayana was found in Ceylon at the end of the sixth century since a copper plaque citing texts of the Greater Vehicle was discovered in the Vijayarama stupa at Anuradhapura. It can be seen that it is difficult to discover the exact part of India Javanese Buddhism came from as there were many possible sources and once established Buddhism evolved in its own way. This is apparent in the *Sang Hyang Kamahayanikan*, the oldest parts of which were written in the first half of the tenth century. It is usually agreed that the Buddhism described in this text must be close to the form practised in Borobudur.

A Cambodian inscription, also from the first half of the tenth century, can possibly give further information about the religious milieu of Borobudur. This inscription is the one engraved on the door jambs of the main door leading to the central sanctuary of Bat Cum in the Angkor area. This temple was Mahayanist. Like Borobudur, it was built after the design of a yantra which remained carved in the temple. The first verse of this text, following Coedès' translation, runs 'May the Buddha give you the Boddhi by which was taught the excellent doctrine denying existence of the individual soul and enabling identification with the universal soul'. Coedès detected Sivaite influence in this verse. Subsequently, Bhattacharya wrote an exegesis of this text in which he shows that its author believed that deliverance was neither annihilation nor a movement from earthly pain to celestial happiness but the liberation of all the limitations of the empirical world, passing from the limits of the finite to the wealth of the infinite. The architecture of the monument tries to express this, and is perhaps conceived to show the search for Nirvana by the believer to achieve the unborn, the unproduced, the uncreated and the unformed beyond reality.

3

The Architectural Setting

〰〰〰

THE architectural setting in which Borobudur was created has almost entirely disappeared. There remain, however, three sources of information about it; firstly, contemporary or earlier monuments which still exist today, secondly, the architectural illustrations on the bas-reliefs of Borobudur and, thirdly, architectural treatises in Sanskrit.

EARLIER OR CONTEMPORARY MONUMENTS

The monuments built before or at the same time as Borobudur are few and mostly Hindu. Because of this they are different in type and designed for different rites. However, they present, both technically and decoratively, some interesting points of comparison. Those which can be dated epigraphically will be considered first.

An inscription dating from 732 commemorating the erection of a lingam on a mountain by King Sanjaya has been discovered on Gunung Wukir, a hill near the road from Yogyakarta to Borobudur. Part of the stele was found in a shrine, Candi Cangal, and another part a little further up the hill. It is generally agreed that the temple mentioned in the stele and Candi Cangal are the same. However some scholars, particularly Vogler, think that the monument is distinctly later than the stele. The temple consists of a main sanctuary, now almost entirely destroyed, surrounded by three small sanctuaries. These consist of a base with a balustrade surrounding a statue raised on a pedestal in the open air.

The next monument chronologically is Candi Kalasan, located in the village of the same name between Prambanan and Yogyakarta. A stele

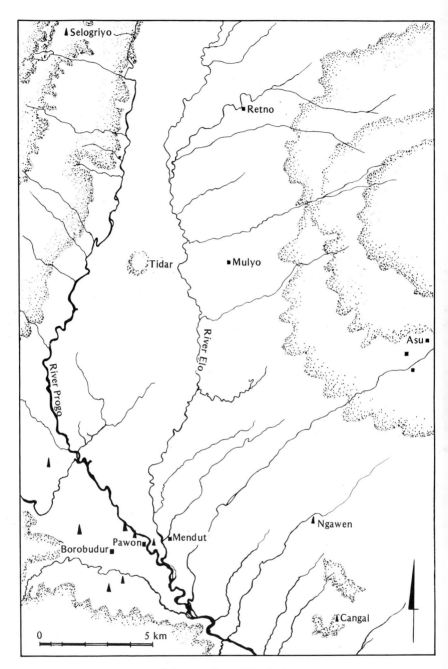

3. Surroundings of Borobudur

discovered near the present temple dates from 778 and commemorates the construction of the Buddhist temple dedicated to the goddess Tara. The temple as it is now is not the original building, but a third construction, completely covering the first two. However, something is known about the original building, since archaeologists have uncovered the base of the first monument under the north-west corner of the present building (A in Figure 6). Two other Buddhist monuments can be linked with original inscriptions. Firstly, near Prambanan, Candi Lumbung, usually associated with the stele of Kelurak, dating from 782, celebrates the erection of a statue to Manjusri, a distant future Buddha. Then there is Candi Sewu, near Candi Lumbung and Prambanan. An inscription dating from 792 was found on the site. It is probable that this inscription, which is very difficult to read and to translate, only concerns an enlargement of the temple. Bosch has shown that Candi Sewu was an expression of a mandala in relief, particularly the Vajradhatu mandala. This temple comprises a main sanctuary surrounded by two hundred and forty small sanctuaries.

Other monuments can be associated with undated inscriptions but paleographically they can be linked to the others; this is the case with the small sanctuaries on the Dieng plateau which can be associated with ancient inscriptions that can still be seen on the plateau. Some of them are written in an alphabet very close to that used by the Pallava dynasty (of the middle of the seventh century) which reigned in southern India on the east coast. Other written inscriptions in different scripts are dated, the most recent being 1210. This shows one thing for certain: there was, for five centuries, a great deal of religious activity on the plateau, but it does nothing to help date precisely the different temples. It is generally agreed that the earlier date is correct (only Bernet-Kempers makes some reservations, though still keeping the earlier date). The monuments are grouped into two styles, the 'old Dieng style' (650 ± 730) which includes the sanctuaries Arjuno, Semar, Srikandi and Gatotkoco and the 'new Dieng style' (730 ± 800), with the sanctuaries Pentolo, Sembodro and Bima. Bima is the only one which shows a technical change in its construction. The old style is very sober and the newer style is more elaborate, though the ensemble remains extremely homogeneous. On this plateau the earliest drainage canal still existing in Java is to be found. As the Dieng plateau is surrounded by a continuous ridge, probably the rim of an old crater, it was necessary to have a drainage canal if the monuments were not to be flooded in the rainy season. The canal is certainly contemporaneous with the construction of the temples.

Lastly, some buildings can be linked to earlier constructions by their style. This is true of the Hindu temples of Gedong Songo near Ungaran, though Soekmono has shown that they are probably more recent and it would seem that Sanctuary A at Gedong Songo is technically very close to Borobudur. In the same area are the six small Hindu temples of Candi Muncul, and these can also be linked to Dieng.

CANDI SAMBISARI

Two kilometres off the main road between Yogyakarta and Kalasan is the village of Sambisari, in which the temple of the same name is found. It is a temple with a similar plan to that of Candi Cangal, but the building is probably a little later. The temple was covered with a very substantial layer of rubble, probably as a result of a flood. This means that it was found intact and the buildings are still being dug out. The central sanctuary is raised on a terrace surrounded by a balustrade; the cella contained a plinth which covered the foundation well. Archaeologists digging at the site have noticed that some of the statuary had been altered in the past, either because of a change in ritual or else to update the building. There are only three flanking shrines which consist of a small terrace enclosed by a balustrade interrupted by an entrance porch on one side. In the centre of each terrace there was a statue unprotected by any covering structure.

ARCHITECTURAL ILLUSTRATIONS

The architectural illustrations on the bas-reliefs at Borobudur are extensive. They show in a very uneven way an idealization of architecture at the time of the building of the monument. The archaeologist Brandes at the end of the last century demonstrated the real archaeological interest of these illustrations which have been studied several times since then, notably by Parmentier. Only a few examples will be mentioned here, but this documentation has considerable detail and interest.

These representations can be divided into two groups, depending on the main material used, wood or stone. Wooden architecture is more frequently illustrated, with numerous technical details which allow us to reconstruct for the most part a wooden building contemporary with Borobudur. It can be seen that if stone constructions were in part inspired by Indian priests, this is also true of wooden architecture, but in the case of the latter such inspiration is purely formal; however, an influence of Chinese techniques can be distinguished in some buildings. Several centuries before the beginning of the Christian era, the so-called Dong-Son civilization spread as far as Indonesia, bringing bronze-casting techniques. But these techniques were perhaps not sufficiently well assimilated for the making of large bronze drums in the area. Associated with many of these bronze drums, a cowrie receptacle dating from the beginning of the Christian era was discovered recently in an archaeological site in southern China. The cover of this piece is decorated with an architectural illustration on the round bosse; it consists of a house with a roof where the ridge beam is extended by two components at the ends in the form of projecting gables. This very special technique, still used today in Sumatra and Sulawesi, appears on the reliefs of Borobudur, in particular in the lower level on the first gallery, north side, west wing (A and A1 in Figure 4).

Mention has already been made of the ancient inscriptions often being written in a script similar to that used by the Pallava dynasty. This Pallava influence can be seen again in the architectural illustrations, in particular in a relief located on the first gallery, east side, south wing (B in Figure 4). No contemporary wooden architecture of the Pallavas remains in India but the stone temples comprise numerous elements imitating woodwork, resting on stone pillars, figuring lions standing on their hind legs. This last motif is found on the bas-reliefs; the lions seem to support sections of wooden columns, crowned with capitals that maintain a complete system of beams independent of the building proper.

Masonry buildings are shown with the same attention to detail. The essential monument of the Buddhist religion, the stupa, is often carved on the reliefs (see C, D, E and F in Figure 4). Its form is explained by

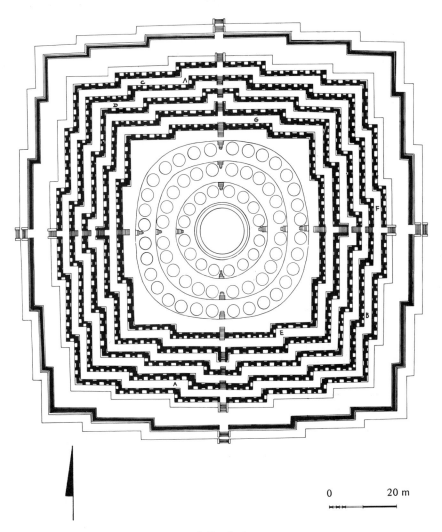

0   20 m

4. Borobudur

the following legend. A king asked his architect what form he intended
to give to the stupa he was about to construct. The divine architect,
Visvakarman, inspired the master craftsman who filled a gold vase with
water. He took some water in the hollow of his hand and then threw it
hard onto the water still inside the vase. A large bubble like a crystal
ball was formed. 'That is how I shall do it,' the architect is said to have
declared. Foucher emphasized in this story its moral side; 'Man who
considers the world like a bubble, like a mirage, will not be noticed by
the king of death' and Mus keeps the cosmogonic aspect, referring to
traditions concerning the cosmic egg which rises above the surface of
the waters.

This legend and also the moral and cosmogonic interpretations explain the different forms of the stupa, which can be almost spherical (C
in Figure 4) or alternatively very squat (D in Figure 4). Most frequently
it is shown as a flattened half-dome resting on a cylindrical drum (E and
F in Figure 4); this is the form of the central stupa at Borobudur but
the silhouette of the pierced stupas on the circular terraces does not
appear in the bas-reliefs.

Some temples are also shown in these reliefs. Their religious persua-
sion can be seen from the decoration on the top of the roof. Buddhist
temples are capped with stupas and Sivaite temples with a trident. In
the fourth gallery, north side, west wing (G in Figure 4) can be seen
two temples situated next to each other; one is Sivaite and the other
Buddhist. The form of these two buildings can be compared to Candi
Arjuna in Dieng.

ARCHITECTURAL TREATISES

It has been noted that the Hinduization of the archipelago was
brought about by priests. Their influence is shown not only in the ritual
necessities required of the architecture and in the symbolism of the
monuments, but also in the purely architectural part of the temples;
this was possible through the architectural treatises brought by these
priests. Comparisons between the texts and the temples have been attempted, in particular between the *Manasara* and the temples in Dieng,
by Bosch, and between the siting of Borobudur and the methods proposed in the *Manasara* by Mus. If none of these studies is very conclu-

sive, it is because the texts do not allow for an exact juxtaposition with the architecture. They are not really architectural treatises but rather like memoranda, for the most part strictly formal. But in these very dense texts appear technical formulae, the ritual importance of which is underlined. So that in the *Mayamata*, in the chapter dealing with the cutting of lingas, it is stated that one of the sides of the stone must be marked so that the linga will be raised in the same position as that in which the stone was found before its extraction from the quarry. This injunction was not strictly followed.

For the establishment of the foundations, where the ritual importance is very great, the temple must face a clearly determined direction. This requires that the cardinal points be defined in a very exact manner. The *Manasara* proposes the following method; a stake (a gnomon) is fixed vertically in the earth, and taking the base of the stake as the centre, a circle is drawn whose radius is equal to the height of the stake. In the morning, when the shadow of the top of the stake touches the circle, the point is marked and in the evening, when the shadow touches another point on the circle, the same thing is done. These two points clearly indicate the east-west direction. Other marks allow one to build more or less exactly the main geometric forms, though some buildings proposed are absurd and those the least useful as far as the architecture is concerned are included. In fact, the authors of these texts try to anticipate as many problems as possible. This is particularly true of the cornice for which a very large number of mouldings is suggested, but in this considerable mass only a few examples were followed, and very freely at that, because in general only the height of the moulding is indicated without the depth. A large part of the text is lyrical and serves only to bolster the imagination of the master-builder.

The architectural setting in Java at the time of the construction of Borobudur was influenced by two movements. One was popular, and most of the houses were built under this influence, using wood almost exclusively. This movement received few outside influences, except for the probably very old Chinese influences in the matter of beam-laying and, more recently, tiling, which seems to be contemporary with the T'ang dynasty. The other movement led to a learned kind of architecture with numerous outside influences which are essentially formal; the materials used were wood and stone or brick. The construction techniques were often local inventions with very few foreign influences. However there are some original Singalese techniques in so far as stone cutting is concerned; but the effort required in the construction of such huge ensembles as Candi Sewu and Borobudur brought about much progress, with techniques being exported to Cambodia and then to India. The formal influence is, however, important. Essentially it probably comes from southern India and appears in the cornice and the pillars of wooden temples. However, there was no direct transposition; for example, the pillars in the shape of a lion, of Pallava origin, are linked with wooden structures which do not seem to relate with what is known of Pallava beamwork.

When Borobudur was begun, Candi Sewu was a builders' yard, Candi Kalasan in its second period of construction and the temples mentioned above were quite new. Borobudur was thus created in an architectural setting of great artistic wealth and in full evolution.

4

The Architecture of the
Monument

CRITIT

THE site chosen for the construction of Borobudur was doubtless
selected for several reasons. The first of these would be human; it
was necessary to construct a building of this importance in an area with
plentiful labour. It is therefore probable that indirectly the fertility of
the River Progo basin played a part in attracting a fairly large popula-
tion. The religious conditions also had to be such as to permit a Buddhist foundation; in spite of the considerable tolerance of Hinduism, it
is difficult to conceive of such a signal manifestation of Buddhism in an
essentially Sivaite environment. It is thus most likely that the site was
selected in relation to the importance of existing Buddhist communi-
ties. A stele has been found at Kalasan dating from 778, erected in
commemoration of the founding of a temple to Tara, and when the
Dutch restorers started to clear Candi Mendut, they discovered that it
was built over an older brick building. The first Mendut was doubtless
already Buddhist and existed before Borobudur. Near the foundations
of Borobudur, de Vink excavated a number of brick funerary stupas,
and what appears to be the remains of a similar stupa has been discovered from a boring carried out on the side of the hill beneath the monument in deposits formed by stone waste coming from the construction
of the monument. Still embodying a fragment of human hip-bone, the
brick casing was in all respects similar to the bricks at Mendut. However
this stupa must have been relatively close to the period of the construction of Borobudur, as many of the monuments in the area were Sivaite.

Stutterheim has noted that the monument was sited at the junction
of two rivers, the Elo and the Progo, doubtless to evoke the most sacred

confluence of all, that of the Ganga (Ganges) and the Yamuna (Jumna). The desire to seek a replica of the holy places was not particular to Java. The need for an ideal Buddhist geographical site led in Angkor to the construction of the temple of Neak Phean, representing the source of the holy rivers of India. It is therefore possible that, in a similar way, the proximity of the confluence of the two rivers helped to determine the choice of the site. The existence, to the north-east of the monument near present-day Magelang, of the hill known as Tidar, the head of the nail which fixed Java in the sea, also perhaps played a part.

Geologically the hill consists of volcanic tuff which is weathered on the surface to form a variable thickness of yellow clay. This soil is not very suitable for building operations and contained hollows with projecting rocks. The first thing which had to be done was to level the site. The natural soil was covered with a layer of brown clay. After these preparations the overseers proceeded to their first pegging out of the ground. The monument is not placed in the centre of the plateau but is slightly to the west, leaving a broad space to the east. It is furthermore not sited exactly between the northern and southern sides of the plateau, as the space to the north is notably bigger. This last particularity was certainly due to the configuration of the original site which is much more sloping to the south than to the north and consequently the monument could not be centred exactly.

THE FIRST PERIOD OF CONSTRUCTION

On the first marking out a small wall of three or sometimes four carefully edged courses formed the foundations of Borobudur in its first form. As will be seen, the foundations were relaid on the outside on two occasions. The foundation wall was partly covered by debris from waste stone. The stone used throughout the monument is andesite, most likely collected in the nearby rivers where different volcanic eruptions had carried down large quantities of variously shaped rocks. After the completion of the foundation wall, the next step was the definitive foot which was somewhat set-off from the foundation wall; the two foundation lines have several differences between them. The projection is 16 cm on the north-east corner while it is only 8 cm on the south-west; this is doubtless correcting errors from the first foundations. The sides of the temple are perfectly oriented: the means used to fix the cardinal points are not known but the foundation was probably done from the two perpendicularly oriented axes, on which were drawn perpendicular lines. At the cross point of these the corners of the monument were sited. The base of Bubrah temple, dating from the very beginning of the ninth century, near Prambanan, had these axes and these perpendiculars carved before the cella walls were built.

As the building progressed, a scaffolding became necessary. It was put into position above the first level of stone waste and the feet of the poles became gradually buried by refuse from the construction. When the walkways began to be paved, the scaffolding remained in place for some time, doubtless until the monument reached the level of the first gallery; at this point the scaffolding was taken away and the space previously occupied by the poles was filled with stone blocks. The beginning of this construction work was not without technical troubles. After laying the first course of the retaining wall for the second gallery, a major subsidence occurred on the west side, doubtless because the fill had been badly compacted. It became necessary to realign the level of the base of the wallfacing; this was done with a levelling course of wedge-shaped stones, which levelled up the base line for the wall.

At the level of the third gallery, a structure was built about which little is known. It was probably almost completed, the proportions and cornice outline and the reliefs mostly begun, before it was completely destroyed. The existence of this structure is known from two facts. According to the borings made for geological research, there emerges at the level of the third gallery inside the monument a relatively narrow area where the infill was very tightly compacted, indicating a working area which must have been in use for some time. Secondly, under the big north stairway which gave onto the foot of the monument and dating from the second period of construction, a large number of carved architectural elements, including cornices and pinnacles, have been discovered. All this debris did not belong to the present building, even though it came from a building whose outline was very similar. There existed then at the end of the first period of construction a complete monument which included a foot which is now hidden, the two first galleries and a central structure since destroyed. The sides of the hill were doubtless arranged in steps which must have been interrupted on each of the axes by the stairways, the siting of which had been laid out but the masonry work not yet begun.

The monument remained in this state a fairly short time, probably less than twenty-five years, because, apart from the well-compacted surface layer, the infill was not yet stabilized and subsidence, which might have been the cause of the resumption of the work, began.

THE SECOND PERIOD OF CONSTRUCTION

The earth movement is especially noticeable on the axis of the north side of the monument. The layer of stone debris slipped and a large gully appeared in the hillside. This is why, quite naturally, the supervisor spurned the parts of the structure destroyed on the northern side. This second period of construction was a complete renewal of the building, while seeking to keep its unity. However, the new plan for the third and fourth galleries shows slight differences. The stairways had to be reconstructed as the structure of the first period was lower and consequently the stairways were less steep. For the new plan it was necessary to redesign them and to rebuild the arches that covered the entrances which no longer gave access to the galleries. To give a unity to the monument new entrance jambs were put onto the old reliefs which were similar to those on the third and fourth galleries. At the same time work was resumed at the base of the monument; a massive foot completely obliterated the reliefs of the first period and on the sides of the hill a complex grading was begun which included five levels of compressed earth covering the layers of debris that had been produced by demolition and construction. These levels were interrupted to give room for the stone stairways partially raised above each levelling, disclosing the string-walls which were then dressed with stone where they were exposed. The levels were laid out following the layout of the monument in relation to the hill, leaving a large area to the east as in the previous period of construction. This space was still further enlarged by a broad projection on each side of the east stairway. It is not known how these levels ended on the north-west corner where the monument joins the prolongation of the hill. While a fairly large circular structure was being built on the top platform, the work was again interrupted.

THE THIRD PERIOD OF CONSTRUCTION

It is not known in what state the builders of the second period left the central structure but it is likely that before new construction work was begun it was levelled before proceeding to the new structure, doubtless utilizing the concave elements of the upper part of the moulded base of the second stage. The work of this period included the construction of the three approximately circular terraces, the pierced stupas and the central stupa. At the same period the balustrade of the first gallery was modified by constructing niches on the curved moulding of the top of the balustrade to add to the number of Buddhas, as will be seen below. At the base of the monument the foot was given further attention by extending the first level and inserting gutters to remove rain-water to the edge of the earth platform. It would seem that these gutters were extended eastwards along the length of the steps which had been begun to be dressed on the eastern side. This enormous job was only done in outline, though the two upper levels of the east side on the north wing were completed.

THE FOURTH AND FIFTH PERIODS OF CONSTRUCTION

These two last periods of construction were simply improvements to the monument in the course of its existence and in contrast with the previous periods did not modify its plan. They included blocking the space between the open niches on the balustrade of the first gallery, and the insertion of a new series of reliefs on the inside of the first gallery under the moulded top of the balustrade. These reliefs were linked with new entrance doorways and new access stairways inserted after a fashion into the previous structures. At this time the compacted earth steps on the hillsides eroded and the debris fell down the slopes at random except on the eastern side which was always better maintained. Even if the monument continued to be visited for some time, the construction work ceased and the upkeep became ever more neglected. Earth accumulated along the length of the monument to the point of covering the whole of the first level of the foot. The steps and the stairways in the sides of the hill disappeared completely. The galleries

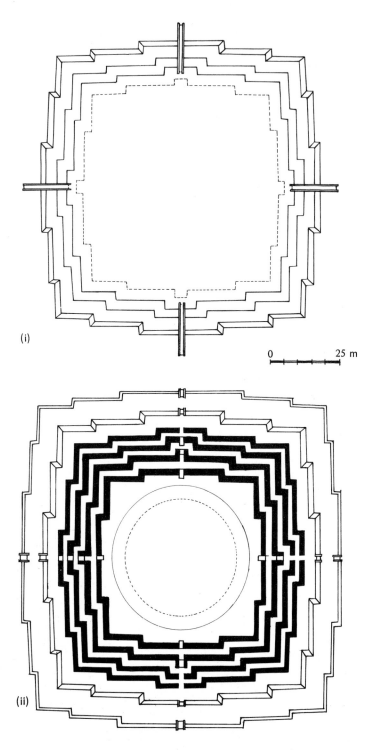

(i)

0   25 m

(ii)

5. Four periods of construction of Borobudur

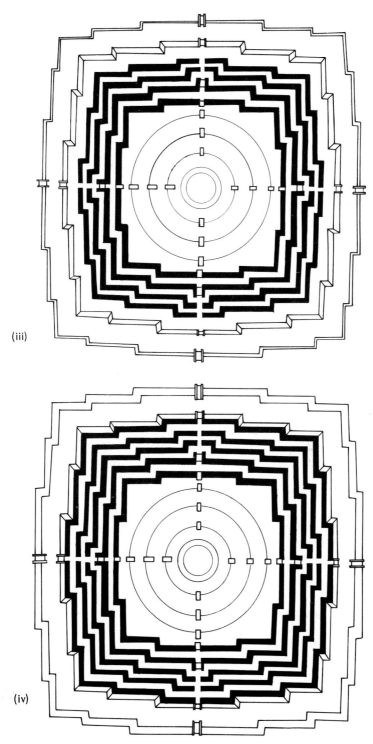

(iii)

(iv)

Continued: Four periods of construction of Borobudur

progressively filled with earth and vegetation invaded the structures which remained visible. Borobudur started its lengthy sleep.

THE TECHNIQUES OF CONSTRUCTION

The construction, with these numerous stops and starts, lasted a period thought to be about seventy-five years. During such a length of time the techniques did not remain unchanged and several modifications in the methods used can be seen. However, in essence, it is a homogeneous construction of stone put together without mortar. Cohesion was consequently obtained internally, using different cuttings to ensure the strength of the building.

Two main types of joints have been noted and they have several variants. The first is a system using right angles, either on the vertical or the horizontal plane; if there were movement the right angles locked into each other, and made for excellent cohesion. In this way whole panels can be seen as having shifted all in one piece. Sometimes, especially in the paving, the right angles were locked into each other with the aid of a forcibly inserted wedge. This last method, probably of Singalese origin, only appeared in Java in the second half of the eighth century, that is, a short time before the beginning of the work on Borobudur. Secondly, a technique using tenons which gripped the mortices was used; this was only used on the monument from the time of the second period of construction.

The stones were linked to each other by double dovetailed clamps. This was not very efficient as the clamps were hewn from the same material which is quite fragile when fairly thin. In Cambodia in the same manner clamps were used to bind the stones but they were generally of metal. The stairways were covered with a cantilever arch, held at the top by a T-shaped key-stone which stays on the last course of the corbelling and goes below the upper level of the course, so assuring a good coherence to the cantilever even when there is movement.

The sculpture was begun *in situ* when the structure was completed. Several unfinished panels give an indication of the techniques used by the sculptors. On appropriately smooth stone, the design was marked out with a chasing chisel and the parts which were to constitute the background were begun first, leaving in relief somewhat convex volumes. Then the sculptor took up the surface again, doing the figures in the foreground and finally the decoration which always remains relative to the attention given to the figures. Finally the whole was covered with stucco which was a simple mortar of lime and sand. Although this stucco at Borobudur has completely disappeared apart from a few very rare places, this is not so at Candi Kalasan where it may still be studied. The stucco covering on this monument comprises two superimposed layers, consisting of the same mixture in the same proportions of lime and the same granule consistency of sand. The first layer is thought to have contained the porosity of the andesite and the second layer could then be moulded more easily since the water used for the composition was not absorbed by the stone; the mortar stayed malleable longer. Doubtless the sculptor touched up the figures once the stucco was completed, which would explain why sometimes the stone carving is only sketched in. It is not known if the monument was painted but it seems likely; the reliefs of the major Khmer monuments were painted in fairly bright colours of blue, red, green and black, enhanced by the application of gold leaf.

THE ARCHITECTURE OF THE MONUMENT

As has been shown, there was no unity of conception to Borobudur and the present state of the monument is an adaptation of an old idea to a new design. So visitors are usually struck by the starkness of the circular terraces which contrasts with the wealth of decoration of the quadrangular galleries. One can see the desire of the supervisors of the third stage of construction to break with what had been initially envisaged at the second stage, namely an outline as rich as the base. The symbolism of the monument, the different hypotheses of which are given in the following chapter, can thus not be presented as a sort of cosmogony where every detail was considered in advance. On the contrary, it would appear that each stage of construction was conceived with a different symbolism.

The description here is of the monument at its peak, that is to say at the end of the third stage of construction when its setting was still intact. The approach to Borobudur was from the east and was without doubt along a path which started at Candi Mendut. This path crossed the River Elo and then led to the edge of the Progo where a small construction existed of which only a few brick elements remain. One crossed the river and Candi Pawon marked a new stage. These buildings are perhaps only parts of a much larger whole surrounding Borobudur with a chain of small temples. The few remains of Wringin Putih two kilometres from the north-west corner point to the remote possibility of such a hypothesis. The main entrance was thus from the east; indeed it has already been noted that the monument was shifted fairly marked-ly to the west on a terrace reached by a vast stairway 4 m wide (the steps were fairly steep, being 22 cm high with a depth of 25 cm). The starting point for the east stairway has unfortunately entirely disappear-ed but a similar stairway was constructed on each of the axes of the monument and the point of departure of the north stairway has been relatively well-preserved. It consisted of a small platform composed of rough ashlar supporting a paving decorated with lions. The variations in level between this platform and the terrace differed according to the axes and brought about modifications in the width of the stairways; the longest extension is to the south where the drop is 12 m, while it is only 7 m to the west and 10 m to the north.

The importance of the variation in level of the southern stairway which ends at the side of a fairly large depression has given rise to the idea that this could have been a pool. However a study has shown that the vegetation found in the lower depths of the depression was not aquatic. It is possible this space was one of the sources of the fill. All the steps of the stairways are of stone and rest on rough ashlar lying on a layer of sand and the debris of stone cutting. The east stairway is bordered by steps projecting from the terrace alignment which is cross-ed by four paved paths constructed in the same way as the stairways. These paths lead to the base of the monument proper, the foot of which is not strictly symmetrical. The northern half is slightly larger than the southern half but the differences are slight. It is thought that the displacement to the north was introduced in the second construc-tion stage. The first gallery is completely symmetrical but when the new foot was added it followed a new base line with a slight displace-ment to the north of 20 cm. If these variations are not great it is because the new construction had to be incorporated in an older struc-ture, and it can be seen that the supervisor of the second stage, when he was freed from the constraints imposed by the walls of his predecessors, noticeably increased the dissymmetry. The retaining wall of the last terrace is off course by 50 cm to the north, which is similar to the shift in some Khmer temples (40 cm at Ta Kev and 43 cm at the Bayon). The circular terraces were approximately centred on the last quadrangular platform. This caused the axes of the stairways to be displaced and they are not in the prolongation of the entries leading from the galleries.

The monument is only a framework for the sculpture. It is essentially a carved ensemble and architectural values play a minor role. This is reflected in the techniques of construction which seek more to give a coherence, to find the form of the original stone, than to try to overcome the mass of the building by extending the architectural space. However the purely architectural difficulties of movement of people, the time it takes to go round and the removal of rain-water played a part in the composition independently of all symbolism. The problem for the different supervisors was that they had to spread the reliefs to the length required by the illustration of the text and one had to read the text, that is, the galleries had to be sufficiently wide so that a panel in relief could be seen at one glance. This decided the width of the gallery and in some degree its development. It is not impossible that some of the panels are padding; one could maintain, in spite of the beauty of the carving, that the scene of Queen Maya's journey to the Lumbini garden is not essential to an understanding of a visual illustration of the life of the Buddha. Without such scenes the continuity of the gallery would otherwise have been difficult to arrange. The reading of the reliefs was done from the east, keeping the monument to the right; when the reading of one gallery is completed, one is back to the beginning. Only one stairway, the eastern one, is used to go up. This stairway must have been somewhat crowded when there were many pilgrims. The galleries become increasingly narrow as one goes higher, which implies that either the upper galleries were crowded or that one moved more quickly as one got near the top. The platform supporting the circular terraces probably served as a clearing space for visitors and it is thought its huge dimensions have perhaps no other reason. One went down by any stairway, undoubtedly avoiding the eastern one which was crowded with people going up. The stairway most likely to have been used for going down is the western one, leading to the monastery. The removal of rain-water was, as has been noted, foreseen at several junctures. The system was very simple; gargoyles were placed at the diagonals of the monument, bringing the water down from one level to the one below as far as the first gallery, where the water on the foot was collected at the base of the first level in a gutter surrounding the monument. Other gutters took the water to the edge of the earth platform. In spite of the heavy rainfall of 1 800 mm a year, this system remained efficient as long as the monument was stable, but as soon as the first movement occurred, the gargoyles did not disperse the water which seeped through the infill and hastened the ruin of the whole.

THE FOOT

The second foot, which hides the first, comprises two steps of very unequal widths. The lower step is uniformly 2.35 m wide. The upper level which forms a large platform 6.75 m wide was surrounded by a very low balustrade, pierced at the bottom with a number of openings for the rain-water to flow through. This balustrade is now almost completely destroyed, though a few sizeable parts remain at the north-west corner of the monument. These two levels were interrupted on the four axes by the stairways, sometimes projecting above the level of the structure. Where this is so they have decorated ramparts on either side. At the top of the rampart where it was flat, a lion's head appeared to disgorge the balustrade which ends at the base either in a spiral scroll or in a Makara head with its open mouth clasping a lion with one paw raised. A richly carved cornice decorates the hidden foot, the plinth of which is decorated with 160 reliefs illustrating the *Karmawibhangga*. This text describes the doctrine of the causes and effects of good and evil. About forty of these reliefs (the exact number is not known because of the damage caused by the building of the added foot) are topped with a brief description in Old Javanese but written in Sanskrit letters. These inscriptions have been translated by Krom; their meaning is related to the relief but in a very indirect way, for example, 'the evil faces' or 'the offering of the parasol' or 'the banner'. They are sometimes interpreted as being an indication for the sculptor since in all probability they would have disappeared beneath the stucco. It would seem that these inscriptions are like those in the gallery of the heavens and the hells in Angkor Wat, dating from the twelfth century, which are placed in the middle of the sculpture and were certainly carved after the sculptor had finished his work. These few words may have served as a cue to the person guiding visitors around the stupa. Above the plinth a broad curved moulding is found, together with other elements culminating a final upper ledge or torus. In this convex moulding the concave moulding, or cyma, was inserted making the link between the added foot and the older structure.

THE FIRST GALLERY

The first gallery is reached by gateways which have now almost completely disappeared, though a few fragments remain to the east and the south. These gateways were constructed with two carved outer facings and rough infilling, a technique which was only used in Java after the construction of the central temple at Prambanan. They can therefore be dated approximately to the middle of the ninth century, and the construction of the gateways and the sculpture of the reliefs tally with this. The gallery itself is composed of the retaining wall of the second gallery and the balustrade stopping the view to the outside. The retaining wall is decorated at two levels with 120 panels each.

The upper level illustrates the *Lalitavistara*, the story of the life of the Buddha from his birth to the sermon at Benares. This series is the most easily understood. Among the numerous panels can be seen the future Buddha, before his birth, informing the gods of his intention to return to earth, his conception in the body of Queen Maya, his birth in the garden in Lumbini, his education, the four decisive encounters with poverty, illness, death and asceticism, the great departure, the hair-cutting, the onslaught of the demons of Mara's army, then the temptations of Mara's daughters and finally the arrival at Benares and the preaching of the sermon.

The lower level illustrates five episodes in the former lives of the historic Buddha; these tales, the *Jatakamala*, were collected in the fourth century. On the inside face of the balustrade can be seen also two levels of reliefs likewise illustrating previous lives of the Buddha but in the north-east corner the panels of the upper level illustrate another text, the *Awada*. This collection of tales relates not to the previous lives of the historic Buddha, but to Bodhisattvas. The last two series of reliefs are either found under the curved moulding or on the backs of the niches opening outwards. Each of these contains a seated Buddha whose symbolical gesture is different depending on the four cardinal points; to the east, the Buddha points his right hand down towards the earth, signifying the calling of the earth as witness; to the south, the Buddha's right hand rests on his knee, the open palm expressing charity; to the west, the two hands are brought flat together one above the other on the lap, palms upwards, symbolizing meditation; and to the north, the right hand is raised, expressing fearlessness. The same arrangement can be found on each of the balustrades of the second, third and fourth galleries. Nevertheless the number of Buddha statues is different:

first gallery	104 Buddhas
second gallery	104 Buddhas
third gallery	88 Buddhas
fourth gallery	72 Buddhas
	368 Buddhas

On the second, third and fourth balustrades all the space which could be turned into niches is used, but this is not so for the first gallery where 120 niches could have been placed, though only 104 have been built, doubtless in order to arrive at the precise total of 368 which has many symbolic meanings whereas the number 384 has none.

Externally under all the niches and the ogee moulding the balustrade is decorated with panels enlivened by feminine deities alternating with groups of apparently demoniac persons.

THE SECOND, THIRD AND FOURTH GALLERIES

The upper galleries comprise the same elements, the retaining wall of the next level and a balustrade. The retaining wall which forms the base of these three galleries is decorated with a single level of reliefs illustrating, on the second and third galleries, the *Gandawyuha*, considered to be one of the most important Buddhist texts. It describes the search for wisdom by Sudhana, the son of a merchant who wishes to acquire great knowledge and to do so meets a large number of Bodhisattvas among whom can be noted, on the reliefs on the third gallery, the Maitreya, the next Buddha. Naturally the scenes on all three are very similar, showing Sudhana in conversation with one of his spiritual masters. They are not easily identifiable and the significance of many of the panels remains conjectural. But it is certain that the supervisors in charge of the monument attached much importance to this text; they gave over 488 panels to it, whereas, as has been seen, 120 were enough to illustrate the *Lalitavistara*. The panels on the upper galleries are spread out not only on the retaining wall and the backs of the balustrades of the second and third galleries but also on the balustrade of the fourth gallery. The main wall of the fourth gallery however is decorated with seventy-two panels illustrating another text, the *Bhadratjari*, a kind of long conclusion to the *Gandawyuha*, illustrating the pledge of Sudhana to follow the example of Bodhisattva Samantabhadra. Here again the interpretation of the panels is not always clear.

On the outer wall the decoration of these three balustrades shows some differences from that of the first gallery where the niches are topped with pinnacles, whereas those on the other balustrades have stupas.

THE UPPER PLATFORM AND THE SO-CALLED CIRCULAR TERRACES

The upper platform is surrounded by a fifth balustrade, plain on the inside and similar to the three previous balustrades on the outside. However, the sixty-four niches decorating this balustrade contain Buddhas in the same position on all sides, unlike the other balustrades where the position of the Buddhas is different on each side. The right hand of these Buddhas is raised like those of the northern side, but the first finger touches the thumb in a gesture symbolizing reasoning. This series brings the number of Buddhas to 432.

The first two terraces have pierced stupas and are not strictly circular. They have rather the shape of a square with its edges rounded off. However, the third terrace and the great central stupa are perfectly circular. On the first terrace are thirty-two open-work stupas with lozenge-shaped openings; the plinth of the finial is square. There are twenty-four similar stupas on the second terrace. The third terrace has sixteen stupas which are markedly different; the openings are square and the finial is raised on an octagonal plinth. Each of these seventy-two stupas contains a Buddha statue, the gesture of which symbolizes the release of the Wheel of the Law during the Benares sermon. The two hands are raised to chest level, the right above the left, with the fourth fingers touching. This last series of Buddhas brings the total number to 504.

The main central stupa contains two chambers, one above the other, both empty. At the time of the clearing of the monument in 1842 on the orders of Hartman, the Resident of Kedu, an unfinished statue of the Buddha with the right hand extending down to earth was discovered in an excavation made by treasure hunters.

This statue was at the root of a serious dispute around 1925 between Krom and Stutterheim. In spite of all the interest in the hypothesis of the latter and the support given to him by no less a person than Van Erp, it seems unlikely that this statue came from the lower chamber of the central stupa. Krom thought that it was an unfinished statue which was rejected because it was inconsistent in some way. This is quite likely, as there are other unfinished statues scattered around the monument on which work had obviously been abandoned.

Nevertheless, were the chambers of the central stupa empty? For what reason did the thieves, possibly at the end of the eighteenth century, decide to smash the stupa open? They may have done so as a result of a chance discovery of some precious object in another stupa. There is some slight evidence that the treasure hunters carried off important booty in that they did not carry their investigations further.

CANDI MENDUT AND CANDI PAWON

These two monuments are laid out on the same east-west line. The alignment was probably not accidental, in spite of a slight change of direction on the eastern side to towards the north-east (a privileged direction in Indian architecture). The topographical position as well as the moulding is similar, though on a different scale, with Borobudur, Mendut and Pawon and shows that they are interrelated.

Mendut was built, according to de Casparis, by King Indra on an older brick structure. The temple is raised on a massive rectangular foundation and consists of a square cella preceded by an entrance portico. The cella contains three statues, with the seated Sakyamuni Buddha in the centre teaching the law. At the bottom of the plinth can be seen the Wheel of the Law flanked by two gazelles; this is a reference to the sermon preached in the gazelle park in Benares where the Buddha taught the Law for the first time. To the left is the Bodhisattva Avalokitesvara and to the right another Bodhisattva, probably Manjusri.

The portico underwent some changes about the middle of the ninth century. The double wallfacing technique was used as in the fifth period in the construction of Borobudur. These changes probably caused the east window above the entrance to the cella to be blocked in.

The outside of the monument is decorated with panels representing Bodhisattvas under parasols. These form part of the Mahayana pantheon, among whom are Manjusri and Samantabhadra, who can also be seen at Borobudur. Nearer to eye level are reliefs decorating the outer sides of the string-walls of the stairway, illustrating classical Indian moralities. On the left hand side, the fable of the tortoise and the two ducks can easily be seen. La Fontaine incidentally knew of this tale from a popular version of the *Pancatantra* which Bernier (whose book of 1670 was one of the earliest western publications relating to Indian art) had introduced to him. The other fables are not always so easy to identify; some of them have been interpreted as illustrating the previous lives of Buddha.

Pawon was probably built at the same time as Mendut. It is on a square base and contains a single statue resting against the carved projecting part of the west wall of the cella. The restoration of both Pawon and Mendut at the beginning of the twentieth century makes their architectural interpretation difficult, particularly so with the top of Pawon which seems of doubtful authenticity.

5

The Meaning of the
Monument

❧

IT has been said, by Bosch, Mus and others, that Borobudur provokes discord. The meaning of the monument has been the subject of more than 500 studies so far and some of them contain remarkably polemical opinions. However, all the authors recognize that the monument is the expression of a symbol and even the architects who have somewhat circumspectly dealt with the subject have never doubted this fundamental aspect of the monument, with at least a part of its purpose being to act as an exhibition gallery.

One of the earlier theories was propounded by Hoenig in 1923 who considered the monument to be unfinished and was originally to have been a Khmer *prasat* but that the foundation slipped and caused the building of the added foot. Parmentier pointed to the unlikely proposition of Borobudur imitating subsequent Khmer monuments but, in taking up the proposal of a change of plan in the middle of the construction work, suggested a vast stupa for the top of the monument. Van Erp showed this was unlikely and in his work of 1931 established that the monument had undergone several periods of construction; his first state of Borobudur has the monument without the added foot with the stairways projecting out and giving access to the first gallery.

These three give architectural reasons explaining a resumption of work on the monument involving a change in concept in the middle of construction for technical reasons, namely that movements in the foundations occurred during construction. However, philologists and theological historians have considered the monument such as it is in its present state. The arguments hinge on two points of view; firstly cosmogonical, that is accounting for the whole universe, since in their view the monument was considered as a vast whole from the very first stone, and secondly theological, depending on the relationship of the Buddha statues to each other.

There are a number of difficulties in considering the different theories under these headings. It is difficult to judge the likelihood of the symbols, whether they come from the text of a geometrical drawing. Some theorists, too, out of self-defence, indicate that an element of vagueness in a part of the theory does not distract from the validity of the whole. The often repeated division into the three spheres of Buddhism, Kamadhatu, the sphere of desire, Rupadhatu, the sphere of form, and Arupadhatu, the sphere of formlessness, falls into this argument and the fact that the three are linked in a single monument is explained as illustrating the Javanese dislike of rigid demarcations.

Krom in his work of 1920 concentrated on the reliefs. He demonstrated that the reliefs of the upper level of the first gallery illustrates the *Lalitavistara* and that with few exceptions the illustrations follow very closely the text which has survived. They do not show the life of the historic Buddha after the sermon at Benares and leave out important episodes like the ascent to Nirvana. Krom thought there was never an intention to show the end of the life of the historic Buddha; this is because the Nirvana of the Sakyamuni was not essential for the masterbuilder of Borobudur; what is important is what can be expected of the future, from Maitreya or from Samantabhadra, another of the seventy-two future Buddhas. From this comes the proclamation of the law on the *Gandawyuha* and the importance given to the Maitreya on the reliefs of the third gallery. Krom extrapolated from these conjectures an interpretation of the Buddhism of Borobudur. He underlined the importance of Mahayanism at the end of the eighth century in Java, exemplified in the statues at Mendut (Sakyamuni between the Bodhisattvas Avalokitesvara and either Vajrayana or Manjusri). He considered a belief in the Jinas to be general at the time of the construction of Borobudur and that a special cult existed for the Bodhisattvas and the goddess Tara. He assumed that the Buddhism practised at Borobudur was tinged with Tantrism, which allows a believer to aim for a state of the Bodhisattva in one's lifetime, as opposed to it being in a very distant future, by practising Yoga and adoring the Buddha.

Borobudur was first compared to a mandala, that is, a geometrical diagram to assist meditation, by Zimmer in 1926. Pott took this up and clarified the definition of a mandala as a cosmic configuration, and distinguished between a mandala and a yantra, the latter not showing the divinities of lower rank which surround a god at the centre of a mandala.

Stutterheim, in his thesis of 1929, discussed at length the name 'Borobudur' which for him could be translated as 'hill foundation', though de Casparis in 1950 thought, as seems more likely, that the name comes from the expression 'Bhumian bhara bhudara', translating as 'Mountain of the accumulation of merits of the (ten) states (of the bodhisattva)'; the expression is indeed found, without the words 'ten' and 'bodhisattva', on a plaque dating from 842.

For Stutterheim, the explanation of the shape of the monument is close to that proposed by Zimmer for the mandala. Mus summarizes the theory in this way: 'Borobudur is a magic model of the universe, conceived for the spiritual exercise of the monks. Its square levels, its round terraces and the final stupa symbolise different layers of suprasensitive reality. The hidden foot corresponds to the material world which mundanely surrounds us and the first step in a mystical direction is to go beyond it; hence covering it up represents its suppression.' There have been plenty of critics of this hypothesis and Van Erp showed, in 1931, that the base was not constructed at the same time but on at least two separate occasions.

The meaning of the monument, for Stutterheim as with Krom, is compared to the contents of the *Sang Hyang Kamahayanikan*, previously mentioned in Chapter 2. His proof rests entirely on the arrangement of the 504 Buddhas in the monument. He counts the number of Buddhas on each balustrade and each circular terrace, and believing in the discovery of an incomplete Buddha in the centre obtains the series 1, 16, 24, 32, 64, 72, 88, 104, 104. Explanations for the gaps, after a division by eight, are ingenious and the Buddhas of the quadrangular terraces 2, 3 and 4 are identified with the Jinas, all of which can be recognized by the traditional hand positions (Aksobhya to the east, Ratnasambhava to the south, Amitabha to the west and Amoghasida to the north).

Mus (1932–4) developed the mystical. The hidden reliefs represented the world which the believer had just left and which he still had to tread underfoot. Borobudur contained a secret world and the doorways are supernatural gaps open to the holy who have transcendent powers. De Casparis and Damais (1968) both add to the endless debate on the meaning of the monument.

A new interpretation of the meaning of the monument will not be attempted here but, making use of recent archaeological discoveries, the dismantling of the monument and its architectural history, one can try to indicate the established symbols or those which at least seem likely and those which need to be rejected in the light of new knowledge.

Borobudur is a mandala, that is, an instrument which assists meditation. However, the same figure did not serve for the design of the first two periods of construction. The first mandala used is symmetrical and the second, which was unsymmetrical, was for better or for worse inserted into the existing symmetrical structure.

A change in form and probably in meaning is not special to Borobudur. It would appear that the inscription discovered at Candi Sewu and dated 792 is an expression of a similar transformation which can be seen in the major modifications carried out on its central stupa. Even if the mandalas used are certainly different at Sewu and at Borobudur, the changes probably stem from the same religious movement. So the meaning of the monument is not only multiple in its actual physical appearance but also historical, which makes an interpretation of the architecture even more complex because what can be seen today is only an adaptation of a new idea superimposed on the concrete expression of older concepts.

The construction of the first stage of the added foot must be part of the change in meaning since this structure is unsymmetrical but the size of this first stage is probably due to technical reasons. It has been seen that in the course of construction subsidence occurred which necessitated levelling courses, especially in the west. In the north this movement was accompanied by a movement of the infill and from this arose the decision to build a more important structure than symbolism required. The subsequent additions to the base are likely to be, as Grolier thought, reappropriations of the monument. The last addition is probably contemporary with the construction of the Hindu temple of Prambanan. This shows that not only was the reigning dynasty tolerant, but also that the monument was not perhaps of strictly Buddhist symbolic significance and was attached to the Sailendra dynasty, hence the importance of a reappropriation. However the meaning is essentially Buddhist and is linked more particularly to Mahayanism. It is a double monument, as Mus emphasized; there is an internal monument which is a picture gallery illustrating the doctrine, showing the preaching of the law and the messianic hope which Mahayanism brings in a general fashion for the future. Then there is the external monument expressing the Buddhist theogony following a plan very similar to that given in the *Sang Hyang Kamahayanikan*.

This much appears established but many aspects of Borobudur, in particular the relationship between the monument and Pawon and Mendut, are still left open; though there is certainly some connexion, the exact meaning does not seem to be very clear yet.

All the hypotheses tending to make the construction of the monument a prearranged cosmogony must be rejected. With this must be rejected the theories that each modification and each obliteration to the plan of work was foreseen, together with the idea that the sculpture of the reliefs on the base was undertaken so as to be covered up when barely finished. It is certain that the number of Buddhas has a meaning and that their distribution in the galleries is deliberate (the distribution of the statues in the niches of the first gallery is the best proof) but the figures should not be overworked as the symbolism is not numerical.

1 Prambanan: the Siva temple and the south annexe

2 Borobudur: north-west corner

4 Borobudur: stupa of the second circular terrace

6

Buddhist Architecture in the Ninth Century

౮₩₩౮

I T has been seen that a profound change in the concept of Buddhism very likely took place in Java at the end of the eighth century. Borobudur underwent the important transformations already described, influenced by a text similar to the *Sang Hyang Kamahayanikan*. Bosch has shown that Candi Sewu followed a different tradition, although also associated with Mahayanist Buddhism. He found traces of this concept in Balinese texts and also in Japanese Buddhism. In spite of the considerable differences between Borobudur and Candi Sewu, it would seem that the major modifications carried out on these two temples, as well as on Kalasan, arose from the same doctrinal movement in Mahayanist Buddhism which showed itself in the practical application of a mandala to the temples brought about by the influence of different texts and giving dissimilar results. This new religious impetus was also the reason for the construction of Candi Sari and Candi Plaosan, and it is probably not unrelated to the temples in the second precinct of Prambanan, even though this was a Hindu building.

CANDI KALASAN

At the end of the eighth century, the temple was still in its original form, a simple square cella. The transformation of this plan into a cruciform building followed a concept apparently very similar to the one used for the remodelling of Candi Sewu, which is described below. It concerned the modification of a sanctuary which was, to simplify considerably, a shelter for a statue, converting it into a mandala ex-

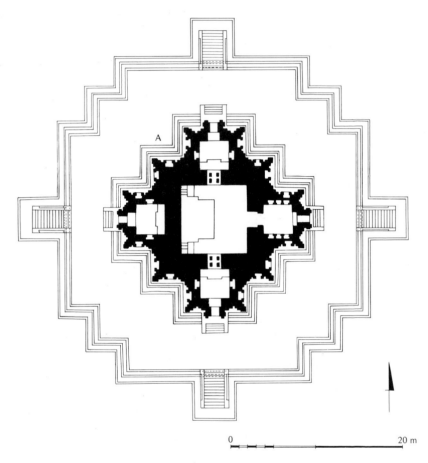

A

0   20 m

6. Kalasan

pressing a theogony. This implies finding room for a much greater number of statues which have to be placed in a given order and accounts for the cruciform arrangement. The second plan was insufficient for this and a third gave new meaning to the monument. It does not seem to be related to Candi Sewu, but to the third period of construction at Borobudur. The capping was transformed and the upper Buddhas and the niches for them were added. Kalasan, at the same time, also underwent a general strengthening. The level of the cella was raised and the base of the central statue modified. The stucco work, which can still be seen in some parts, was added in this third period. The two layers of plastering which can be seen on the masonry do not indicate a restoration but show the use of a different technique mentioned in Chapter 4. The statues have disappeared, except for a few Buddhas on the capping. The statue of the main cella was probably bronze as the support of the mount has traces of metallic oxide.

CANDI SEWU

Candi Sewu means 'a thousand temples' though in fact there are only 240 small sanctuaries in the second precinct. The term probably simply indicates a large number. However, Bosch has noted that the requirements for the mandala are a thousand secondary sanctuaries. It is likely therefore that the modern name unintentionally restores the original nature of the monument. The central sanctuary of Candi Sewu is not in its original state but has undergone a substantial change. In its first form the building was a simple square cella, surrounded by four smaller temples without much connexion with the main building. The transformation involved changing the plan to a cruciform one, by modifying the position of the doorways. The door-frames marked 's' on the plan in Figure 7 were removed. The passages indicated by the letter 'o' in the plan were closed by doors whereas they were left open in the first state of the building, and the doors marked 'f' were narrowed. In this way it can be seen that the niches cut into the external dressing of the wall of the central cella were incorporated into the side sanctuaries. It was also during this modification that the 240 small shrines were built inside the second precinct. They all have the same plan, a square cella with a small portico in front, but they are all different in decora-

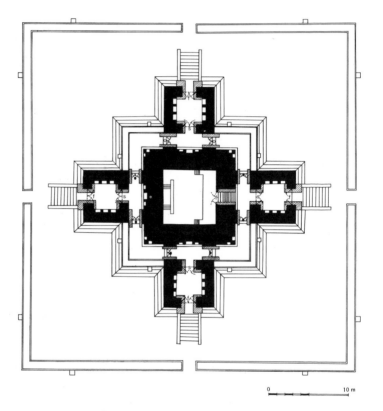

0   10 m

7. Central sanctuary of Candi Sewu

tive detail and in the arrangement of the statues—almost all of which have disappeared. Those which can be seen on the site are not in their original position. These statues are quite similar, in the way they are made, to those at Borobudur. It seems likely that the main statues were of bronze.

Candi Sewu, as mentioned before, cannot be separated from two smaller monuments nearby, Candi Bubrah and Candi Lumbung. Only the base of Bubrah and the elements of the walls of the cella have survived. On the surface of this base the previous tracing of the axis of the walls can be seen. Candi Lumbung is in a better state of preservation and comprises a central sanctuary surrounded by sixteen smaller buildings, rather like those at Candi Sewu. The cella of the central sanctuary is square and opens to the east. The four walls are hollowed out with niches, one to each wall on the south, west and north but two on the east side, on either side of the entrance. The central niche of the west wall is topped with a much smaller niche. This was probably hidden by the ceiling which rested on the cornice and concealed the inner surface of the vault above.

CANDI SARI

The temple of Candi Sari is now reduced to its main sanctuary. It was probably surrounded by buildings and shrines similar to those at Plaosan. It faces east and consists of two levels of three cellas. The upper floor was reached by a wooden staircase located in the south cella (A in Figure 8). The upper cellas were also used for worship and not, as is often repeated by guides, as monks' quarters or a treasury. The statues inside the building have all disappeared. The excellent external decoration consists of female divinities, probably Taras, who are carrying flowers, and of Bodhisattvas with musical instruments, among whom can be seen one playing the lute and another the cymbals. Some of these Bodhisattvas are associated with the planets; the crescent moon can be seen at the south-west corner.

CANDI PLAOSAN

Candi Plaosan is today completely different and very complex. The two main sanctuaries, on the same plan as Candi Sari but opening to the

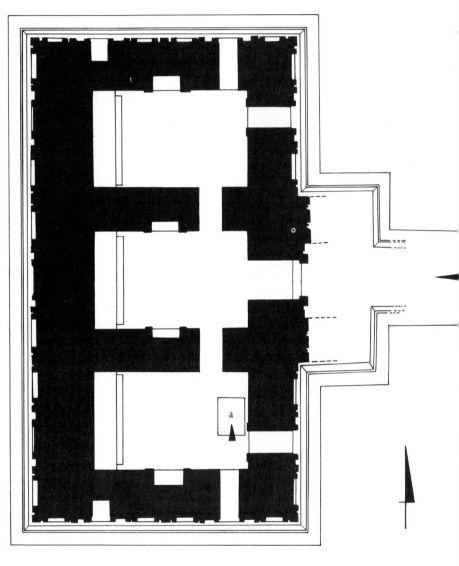

0   5 m

8. Candi Sari

west, are in the centre of two juxtaposed rectangular precincts. Both of these aré enclosed in a courtyard containing 174 small buildings—116 stupas and 58 shrines. A great number of short inscriptions have been found on these buildings which will be discussed later. Two of them mention the gift of a sanctuary by Rakai Pikatan, which allowed de Casparis, who published these texts, to date the gift to between 825 and 850. This date is very close to that of the construction of Prambanan (consecrated in 856) proposed by de Casparis and accepted by Damais. This is not incompatible technically. Prambanan was constructed by a new method which is general to the later Hindu-Javanese monuments and this can be seen in Plaosan, in particular in the main building to the north, where two andesite dressings enclose a very indifferent infill of volcanic tuff. Candi Sari, however, is probably earlier; what can be seen of the base is technically very similar to Kalasan.

In the main temples at Plaosan, the cellas on the ground floor each had a bronze statue flanked by two stone statues. The bronze seated statues, with legs folded, rested on a stone base in the form of a lotus and are all missing. The stone statues represent Bodhisattvas and are nearly all in place. Upstairs, it seems likely that there were statues, but because of the arrangement of the windows there was not, as on the ground floor, a group of three statues but probably only one. The reliefs may well show donors and are found on the inside walls on the ground floor. The traditional representation of a Khmer prince, distinguished by his crown, can be seen in the person carved on the right-hand wall of the northern cella. The divinities on the external walls are not as fine as at Candi Sari and are nearly all male. Only the small personages around the windows are female.

THE MEANING OF THE BUDDHIST MONUMENTS

Bosch identified the mandala which served as the design of the second period of construction of Candi Sewu as the Vajradhatu mandala. This comprises the five Jinas; Vairocana in the centre, Ratnasambhava in the south, Amithaba in the west, Amoghasida in the north and Aksobhya in the east. The main problem in linking the Vajradhatu mandala with Candi Sewu lies in the last figure. It is not possible to place a divinity to the east, since it is in the entrance of the portico of the cella in which Vairocana is to be found. So Bosch places the statues representing the Jinas on the right hand on entering the side chapels, and in the niches hollowed into the walls perpendicular to those of the central cella. This does not correspond to the position of the Jinas indicated in the mandala, where they are found along the axes of the central square containing Vairocana. In spite of this caveat, the identification seems likely. To confirm this hypothesis, small statues in bronze have been discovered at Nganjuk in east Java. These certainly form part of a very similar mandala but centred on Manjusri. Aksobhya is to be found there and most of the Taras in the Vajradhatu mandala.

Candi Sari and Plaosan are also mandalas. This is particularly obvious at Plaosan with the small temples in the second precinct. It would seem that the introduction of a second floor in the central buildings of the temples is an architectural expression of Buddhist tantric mythology. In Chapter 2 it was seen that each Jina is linked to an earthly Buddha and a celestial Bodhisattva. The Bodhisattva would be shown on the ground floor and the Buddha above. This is only a theory partly confirmed, however, by the reliefs of Candi Sari where Taras similar to those at Nganjuk are to be found, namely the Tara carrying flowers, and that playing the cymbals. In spite of so many differences, it would seem that these temples are in large part the expression of many forms of the Mahayanist theogony.

However, the additions to Candi Plaosan by the Sanjaya ruler, Rakai Pikatan, probably corresponds to something else. This particular mandala would seem to represent the kingdom. De Casparis indicated that the inscriptions should be placed geographically, the dignitaries of the west to the west, those of the south to the south and so on. The gifts of the kings would occupy a privileged position in the corners or on the axes of the sides. Although this, in the state of current knowledge of the ancient geography of central Java, is very difficult to prove, it seems very likely. At the end of the first half of the ninth century, not only the temple but the whole kingdom becomes a mandala. One can perhaps see beginning to develop in this identification a political effort on the part of Rakai Pikatan asserting himself over the whole country on becoming free of the Sailendra tutelage. Offering a sanctuary in a temple that represents the kingdom can be seen to be a devout act ensuring merit in the hereafter, and the enrichment of the kingdom itself also becomes a devout act. It is probable that Rakai Pikatan gave expression to a similar idea, but for the consumption of Hindu believers, in constructing the small temples in the second precinct of Prambanan, where de Casparis found some inscriptions in the same geographical disposition as at Plaosan.

This concept of Buddhism, directly adapted to ruling the kingdom, was to be richly illustrated much later at the beginning of the thirteenth century by the Khmer king, Jayavarman VII, who, with the Bayon, constructed an ideal vision of the kingdom centred around his omnipresent personality.

7

The Hindu Monuments of the Ninth Century

ᐸᑎᕊᑎᕊᐳ

IN Indonesia the Hindu religion took the form of Sivaistic worship. From the existence of a large number of small temples scattered throughout the country, the impression is gained that the ancient social structures were better adapted to Sivaism than Buddhism. Statues of Siva and lingas have been found everywhere, whereas Buddha statues are very rare. Krom drew the conclusion that Buddhism in Indonesia was rather an aristocratic religion whereas Hinduism was the religion of the people.

In the construction of Hindu temples of the ninth century, the outline is on the whole similar to Buddhist architecture, but the techniques and the plan are not the same. The master craftsmen used a new technique to build a wall, raising two parallel retaining walls and filling the space between with different components bound with mud. This technique came from India where it had been employed for centuries. It appeared for the first time in the buildings of the so-called Kulli civilization in Baluchistan, which dates from the second millennium before Christ. Because of this, it would seem that the temples, from about A.D. 830 onwards, follow an Indian model which is markedly different from the model of previous Hindu temples in Indonesia. It corresponds to a new Indian impetus, both doctrinal and technical, perhaps brought about by Islamic pressure in India, which is also to be found in the final modifications to Borobudur in the fifth stage of construction (in the doorways of the first gallery) and in the reconstruction of the entrance portico at Mendut. The plans of the different temples show a singular unity of conception. From the simplest to the most complex the same elements can be found: a central cella which is reached through an entrance porch, the three walls having either a niche or a small chapel. Even the iconography is very homogeneous: in the centre, Siva faces east or west, to his right is Agastya, another representation of Siva in the form of a guru (4 in Figure 9), behind him Ganesha, his son, with the elephant head (3 in Figure 9) and on his left is Durga, his wife, who is killing the demon (2 in Figure 9). Two temples only will be described here; one is very simple, Candi Asu, but the other, Candi Prambanan, is extremely complex and shows the quintessential temple in all its symbolic wealth.

CANDI ASU

Candi Asu is found near the road linking Mungid and Boyolali, passing between the two volcanoes Merapi and Merbabu. It was all built at the same period on levelled ground. After the pegging out of the ground giving it its orientation, the builder designed two concentric squares on which he built a wall of hewn stones. The external wall forms the dressing of the base of the temple, the internal wall the central pit which was built for the foundation deposit (1 in Figure 9). The space between the walls has been filled to a height of about 2 m with stones loosely held together with earth. At this level the whole was covered with paving, keeping the space, above the internal square for the central statue. On the west, a mass of masonry was brought up against the outside wall and forms the base of the access stairway. Then, on the paving, a new layout was traced, adapting to the irregularities of the work done up to then. This marking out gives the two axes of the temple cella; the perpendiculars were drawn from the axes. The construction of the temple proper probably began at the angles because it is on the angular blocks that the whole structure rests. When the temple was by and large completely finished, the outline carving began from the top. Then the details were filled in, starting at the top. Large pieces were left until later, particularly lintels which had to be sculptured in the round. This work remains incomplete. Finally the statues were put into place. They were not carved into the monument and were movable, which explains why they have disappeared.

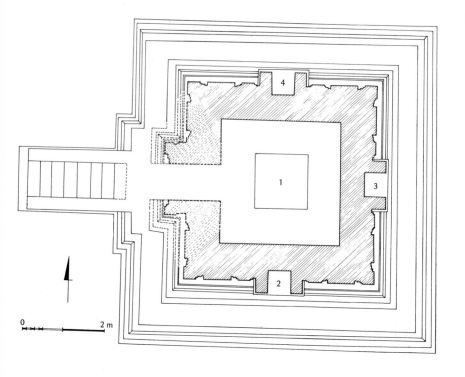

9. Candi Asu, a typical Hindu temple

CANDI PRAMBANAN

De Casparis established that an inscription dated A.D. 856 in the Jakarta Museum, but the exact source of which is unknown, commemorates the consecration of the Prambanan complex. The text contains a description of the temple. An extract of de Casparis' translation follows:

... 15/ A beautiful dwelling for the God . . .; at the gateways, two small buildings were erected, different in construction; there also was a Tanjung tree . . . together (?) beautiful were the numbers of small buildings to be used as hermitages, which might, in their turn, be an example. . . . 25/ After the Siva sanctuary had been completed in its divine splendour the (course of the) river was changed so it rippled along the grounds; there was no danger from the wicked ones, for they had received their due; then the grounds were inaugurated as temple grounds. . . .

The passage 'There was no danger . . . their due' is probably an allusion to the consecration of the temple grounds. This first phase of the rite is shown by small buildings placed at the nine essential points forming the courtyard. These were the centre, the corners and the middle of the four sides; the square is not in fact exact, as the south side is 112 m but the north side 108 m long. The main tower is placed next to the base of the central small building and was shifted slightly to the north, so that it does not cover the place where evil spirits, disturbed by the construction, had been appeased by offerings. Similar small buildings were built symmetrically on each side of the stairways, but, unlike the buildings for ritual use, have no openings.

The temple, sometimes known as Candi Lara Jonggrang, comprises three enclosures. The first is that of the consecration and is oriented to the four cardinal points. The second is also square, 225 m on each side, and follows the same orientation. The third is on the same square plan, 338 m a side, but does not follow the same orientation as it is angled towards the north-east. Only the first two enclosures are concentric. Inside the outer courtyard the River Opak was probably changed in its course as the inscription of 856 indicates.

The second enclosure contains 224 small ruined structures, arranged in four concentric rows, called the Candi Perwara. It is not known for certain if they were ever completed. Two of them have been reconstructed, one on the east side and one at the north-east corner. The doorway of each of these sanctuaries faces outwards; the temples on

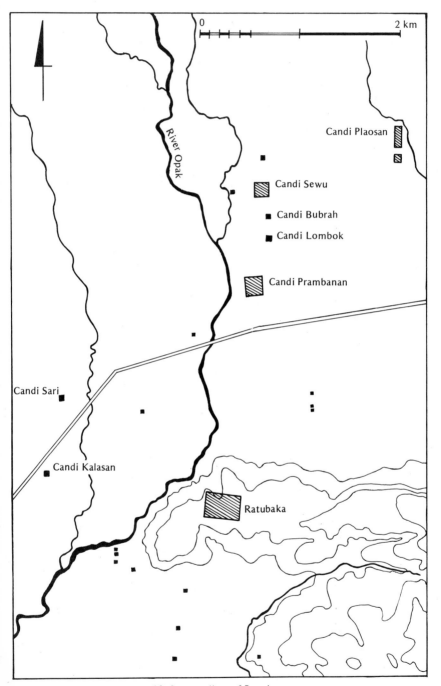

10. Surroundings of Prambanan

the south side open to the south, those on the west to the west and so on (in Cambodia, however, in similar arrangements of the same period the doorways all face east, even when this opens onto a wall). The shrines on the diagonal lines have two entrances; for example, the shrine at the north-east corner opens to the east and the north. So that whatever side one looks at, the first row has twelve doorways, the second fourteen, the third sixteen and the fourth eighteen; as a result of this arrangement there are a total of sixty doorways opening onto any one side. As the inscription says, 'beautiful were the numbers of small buildings'.

The central courtyard has the three main temples, dedicated to the Hindu trilogy, Siva in the centre, surrounded by Vishnu to the north and Brahma to the south. The temple of Siva is formed by a central cella opening to the east; this is flanked by three smaller cellas consecrated to the usual gods, Agastya to the south, Ganesha to the west and Durga to the north. This cruciform plan is very difficult to complete as the builders chose to keep the same arrangement right up to the top. This leads to a vertical angularity which, at the top, is not completely satisfying. Facing the three main buildings are three smaller sanctuaries opening to the west. The shrine of the central building is dedicated to Nandin, the bull which serves as Siva's mount. The temples to the north and south were cleared after their statues had already disappeared. It is likely that Garuda, the mythical bird which transported Vishnu, was to the north and to the south the Hamsa, the goose on which Brahma rode. A host of statues completed the iconography of the different shrines. For example, in the sanctuary of Vishnu, in addition to the central statue which is still in place, a statue has been discovered which shows Vishnu carrying his wife Laksmi, another showing him in the shape of an ugly dwarf and a third in the form of the lion-man Narasimha.

Under the central statues, the pits were hollowed out; these play an important part in the symbolic function of the temple. Under the statue of Siva, the pit goes to a depth of 16 m and reaches the water-table. Masonry at the bottom enables the water to remain there all the time as in an ordinary well. This arrangement is not unusual. At the bottom of Candi Songoriti, near Malang, a hot water spring even flows through the bottom of the pit and is led away from the sanctuary by conduits. At

Prambanan, above the part for the water the walls of the square are carefully built of hewn stones and filled with earth, mixed with stones, to a depth of 6 m under the ground of the cella. At this point, the whole surface of the square is carefully laid to a height of three courses. In the centre is a space where Ijzerman discovered an urn which contained small pieces of gold leaf cut in the shape of a tortoise, a snake, a circle marked with lotus flowers, and rectangles on which are drawn letters of the Sanskrit alphabet.

Under the other statues the arrangement is similar without, however, reaching water level and sometimes the deposit of gold leaf is just underneath the statue, as is the case with the statue of Vishnu. The urns also sometimes contain sand and ashes.

THE RELIEFS AT PRAMBANAN

The reliefs, carved on the inside of the balustrades of the main temples, are one of the chief attractions of Prambanan. Those on the temple of Siva and Brahma recount the story of the Ramayana. This is not meant to illustrate the Indian text but a Javanese adaptation. The story begins with the panel to the left of the east axial entrance of the Siva temple and the course of the story can be followed by moving first to the south. The gods, tired of the power of the giant Ravana, ask Vishnu to come to their aid to neutralize his influence. Vishnu is reincarnated in Rama, the son of the King of Ayodhya. After different adventures he marries Sita, but a giantess, Curpanaka (Sarpakanaka), falls in love with him. Rama spurns her love and Laksamana, his half-brother, makes the situation irreparable by cutting off Curpanaka's nose and ears. She goes to complain to her brother Ravana, who decides to avenge the insult by carrying off Sita himself; to do this he has to get Rama and Laksamana out of the way. One of Ravana's attendants, Marici (Marica), is changed into a golden deer; Rama, at Sita's request, goes in pursuit of this wonderful beast, thus leaving his wife alone and allowing Ravana to seize her. A garuda who watches the abduction tries in vain to stop it, though Sita is able to entrust him with a ring which he gives to Rama. Rama, to get Sita back again, forms an alliance with the monkeys; one of their leaders, Hanuman, is sent to Ravana's capital, Lanka (identified with the island of Ceylon), to seek information about

1. Borobudur, as seen by Wilsen (1849) (*Borobudur Restoration Project*)

2. View taken from the air from the east (*French National Geographical Institute*)

3. View of the monument from the north-west corner (A.C. Beau)

4. Balustrade of the first gallery, north-east corner (*A.C. Beau*)

5. West stairway (*A.C. Beau*)

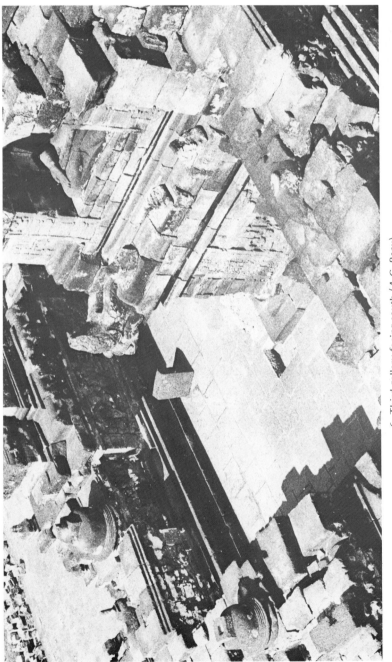

6. Third gallery facing south (*A.C. Beau*)

7. The passageway inside the third gallery (*A.C. Beau*)

8. The north doorway of the fourth gallery (*Borobudur Restoration Project*)

9. A niche in the fifth balustrade facing west (*A.C. Beau*)

10. View from the upper platform looking towards the fifth balustrade (*A.C. Beau*)

11. The first circular terrace (*A.C. Beau*)

12. A Buddha on the first circular terrace (*A.C. Beau*)

13. The central stupa seen from the first circular terrace (*A.C. Beau*)

14. Candi Mendut: Relief of the staircase, the turtle and the two ducks

15. Candi Kalasan: south-west niche, east face

16. Candi Sari: east side

17. Candi Plaosan: south side

18. Candi Plaosan: restored shrine in the southern group

19. Candi Sewu: restored shrine, north-east corner

20. Candi Prambanan: north-east corner of the central sanctuary

Sita. Unfortunately he is discovered, put into prison and condemned to having his tail burned. To carry out this torture Hanuman's tail is wrapped in oil-soaked rags which are set on fire, but at this moment Hanuman escapes and, with his tail alight, sets fire to Ravana's palace and goes off to find Rama. Together they decide to build a dyke to reach Lanka; the sea gods oppose the project at first, but Rama appeases them and with their help the dyke is quickly finished and the monkey army crosses the sea.

The end of the story is taken up on the balustrade of the temple of Brahma and one can follow it by similarly beginning on the east and keeping the balustrade to one's left. These panels tell of the story of the battles Rama fought to regain Sita, but when she was restored to him he noticed she was pregnant. Rama then doubts his wife's virtue and in spite of her protestations of innocence, banishes her to the forest. She gives birth in the wilderness to male twins, Kusa and Lawa. When they reach manhood, at the behest of their mother, they are acknowledged by Rama who is now the King of Ayodhya and who, full of remorse, abdicates in their favour and mounts into the sky, where he resumes the form of Vishnu.

On the balustrade of the north temple stories of the youth of Krishna are to be found; he is also another incarnation of Vishnu. Though the general meaning of these reliefs is certain, the identification of each of the panels is not yet complete.

Finally there is an entrance in the third enclosure, which is still visible, to the south of the temple between the souvenir shops and the artists' entrance to the theatre where Javanese ballet performances inspired by another version of the Ramayana take place. In this, for example, Sita's virtue is tested in a trial by ordeal by fire; the flames recede from her and she is shown to be Rama's faithful spouse.

KRATON RATU BAKA (RATU BOKO)

To the south of Prambanan is a broad hill, on top of which a series of terraces and ceremonial gateways has been built; these served as the foundations and entrances to buildings made of less durable materials. This group of buildings is considered to have been a palace. It is entered by a triple porch which, although it appears to be made of stone, consisted internally of a series of wooden tie beams. The lintels of the doorways are made from small stone blocks which give the appearance of being hewn in a rather more complicated fashion than usual, but in fact each stone is hollow and was backed by a wooden beam, probably a rather roughly hewn tree trunk. The restorers of this entrance have replaced, in most instances, the wooden ties by concrete beams.

The main terraces are reached after passing through the village beyond and to the right of the stone gateways. On them can be seen the bases of pillars which were doubtless the foundations of a pendopo or an open pavilion structure such as can still be seen in contemporary Javanese palaces. In a hollow beside the raised platforms are remains of ancient buildings forming part of an ensemble with pools and surrounding walls and which are called, probably incorrectly, the water garden.

Mention was made in Chapter 3 of Candi Sambisari, which, although of the Prambanan group and Hindu rather than Buddhist, antedates Prambanan in time, being of the eighth century in all probability.

THE MEANING OF THE HINDU MONUMENTS

Archaeologists have for long maintained that the Hindu temple had a funerary purpose. The hypothesis can be resumed thus: when the king or prince died, he was burnt. A part of the ashes was thrown into the sea and the rest kept in an urn or casket made of stone or bronze along with gold leaf or precious stones. The urn was placed in the centre of a temple in a pit made for this purpose. Above the pit a statue representing a god in the form of the dead person was erected and during a ceremony the deity was reincarnated in the statue.

Soekmono has brought this theory into doubt, linking the ceremonies described in the *Negarakertagama* and the current cremations that take place in Bali. He notes that these ceremonies only differ in one respect, the consecration of the image of the dead person in a temple, and that neither in Bali nor in the *Negarakertagama* is there question of the ashes of the body being kept or thrown into the sea. Soekmono then makes the comparison between the deposits in Javanese temples and the *pripih* (offering) in modern Balinese temples. These are made up of five metallic sheets which have magic characters inscribed on them. They are wrapped up in peeled reeds, herbs and cotton and the whole is tied up with red, black and white thread. The offering is then enclosed in a golden casket or one made of silver, stone or porcelain. One offering is placed underneath the temple, and another under the roof-beams of the temple.

A ruined Balinese temple might therefore have an offering like the foundation deposit in ancient Javanese temples. Moreover, even though caskets have been found beneath the statues, it is not the only possible place for them. Consequently, in Candi Selogrio bronze bowls were placed in the stone caskets at the four corners of the base of the temple. There is therefore no particular place for an offering which is not necessarily associated with a statue.

In conclusion Soekmono thinks that the Javanese Hindu temple was not a funerary monument but was a temple representing Mount Meru, the dwelling of the gods. The deposit is the very essence of the temple; it is what gives it life, in much the same fashion as relics give importance to a Buddhist stupa. It is not necessary to keep the ashes of the dead person in the temple in order to erect a statue to the dead person in the shape of a deity. The Khmers erected lingas which symbolized the creative forces of the king during his own lifetime without there being any reason to believe that the temple became a mausoleum after the death of the monarch.

This concept of the Hindu-Javanese temple also corresponds with the number and geographical spread of the shrines. Each village or hamlet had its temple representing Mount Meru, the home of the gods. The cella is simply a symbolic cave in the mountain where the faithful could come to worship their god, who sometimes took on the appearance of a dead monarch.

Conclusion

THE architecture of Indian origin in Java is closely linked to its religious meaning. The techniques used are not designed to improve on architectural volume but, on the contrary, the designers readily acknowledge the laws of gravity. All the same, it is not true that purely architectural considerations were absent from Borobudur and the monuments nearby. This can most easily be seen in the proportion and outline of the cornice. For example, the mouldings on the hidden foot at Borobudur are very powerful. The architect knew how to capture the light on the broad concave and convex line of the moulding which is emphasized by the dark area under the semicircular projecting edge. Beneath this there is deep shadow at any hour of the day because the projection is sufficiently broad. The shadows on the curves of the moulding, however, change according to the time of day and give variety to the surface.

The horizontality of Borobudur has often been remarked upon (particularly by Van Erp and Mus) and is not the work of an insensitive designer. What is perhaps remarkable is that after all its numerous alterations the monument manages to preserve an idea of unity. This was deliberately sought after at the end of the second and third periods of construction when the architect was able to give the impression of there being a single concept behind the building by adding decoration to the cornices and new doorways to the lower galleries.

The architectural forms created at Borobudur did not have time to have much influence since the Hindu expansion came too quickly after the monument was completed. Even if, historically, the reigning princes made an effort not to antagonize the Buddhist community, the

Buddhist movement was spent. Plaosan is the last of the great Buddhist buildings in Java.

If the horizontal lines are dominant in Borobudur, Candi Sari and Plaosan, it is the vertical lines which become of major importance in Prambanan. There the attention is directed to the summit and, perhaps more than at Borobudur, it can be seen what little importance is attached to architectural volume in the way the monument is conceived. With Prambanan it is really a case of reconstructing a mountain. There is no relationship between the size of the cellas and the amount of masonry used in the building. To enhance the apparent height of the building, tricks in perspective were introduced, by reducing the distance between the horizontal bands as one gets nearer the top and accentuating the natural perspective. The moulding has, however, lost much of its importance and strength. The wealth of decoration gives a kind of resonance to the outline, so much so that the upper parts are difficult to distinguish clearly. Though Borobudur had little architectural influence, Prambanan was the model for many temples of the thirteenth and fourteenth centuries in east Java.

With the extension of Islam in central and east Java in the seventeenth century, the Hindu-Javanese period and the structures that went with it came to an end. Hinduism took refuge in Bali and adapted to a smaller architectural scale. A different form of building was required for a mosque and different materials were used, wood or brick replacing stone. But Java has triumphed over its numerous kingdoms and the many different periods in its history. Its syncretic nature is still observable; the Buddha at Candi Mendut and the four principal Hindu statues in Candi Prambanan regularly receive offerings of flowers from local people.

Bibliography

Abbreviations
BEFEO Bulletin de l'Ecole Française d'Extreme Orient
TBG Tijdschrift voor Indische Taal-, Landen Volkenkunde uitgegeven door het (Koninklijk) Bataviaasch Genutschap van Kunsten en Wetenschappen

* * * *

Battacharya, K., *L'Atman Brahman dans le boudhisme ancien*, Paris, 1973.

Bernet-Kempers, A.J., *Ancient Indonesian Art*, Amsterdam, 1959.

Bosch, F.D.K., 'A hypothesis as to the origin of Hindu Javanese Art', *Rupam*, No. 17, Janvier 1924.

———, 'De inscriptie von Kelorak', *TBG*, LXVIII, 1928.

———, *Selected studies in Indonesian archaeology*, The Hague, 1961.

Buchari, 'Preliminary report of an Old Malay inscription at Sodjomerto', 1966 (unpublished note).

de Casparis, J.G., *Inscripties uit de Çailendra tijd* (Prasasti Indonesia I), Bandung, 1950.

———, *Selected inscriptions from the 7th to the 9th century A.D.* (Prasasti Indonesia II), Bandung, 1956.

———, 'New evidence on cultural relations between Java and Ceylon in ancient times', *Artibus Asiae*, XXIV, 1961.

Coedès, G., 'Les inscriptions de Bat Cum', *Journal Asiatique*, CXC, 1908.

———, *Pour mieux comprendre Angkor*, Paris, 1947 (English translation *Angkor*, Kuala Lumpur, 1963).

———, *Les états hindouisés d'Indochine et d'Indonésie*, Paris, 1968.

Conze, E., *Le Bouddhisme dans son essence et son developpement*, Paris, 1951.

Coomaraswamy, A.K., *History of India and Indonesian Art*, 1927.

Damais, L.C., 'Etudes d'Epigraphie indonésienne', *BEFEO*, XLV, 1951, *BEFEO*, XLVI, 1952, *BEFEO*, LVI, 1968.

Dupont, P., 'Les Buddhas dits d'Amaravati en Asie du Sud-Est', *BEFEO*, XLIX, 1958.

Foucher, A., 'Notes d'Archéologie bouddhique', *BEFEO*, IX, 1909.

Groslier, B.P., *Inscriptions du Bayon*, Paris, 1973.

Hoenig, A., *Das Formproblem des Borobudur*, 1924.

Ijzerman, J.W., *Beschrijving der Oudheden nabig de grens der residentie's Soerakarta en Djogdjakarta*, about 1880.

Krom, N.J., *Archeological Description of Barabudur*, The Hague, 1927.

Lamotte, E., *Histoire du Bouddhisme indien des origines à l'ère Saka*, Louvain, 1958.

Le Bonheur, A., *La sculpture indonésienne au Musée Guimet*, Paris, 1971.

Leemans, C., *Boro-budur dans l'île de Java*, Leide, 1874.

Macdonald, W., Review of Van Erp *Beschrigving van Barabudur*, *TBG*, LXXII, 1932.

Moens, J.L., '*Barabudur, Mendut en Pawon un hum onderlinge samenhang*', *TBG*, LXXXIV, 1951.

Mus, P., 'Barabudur, esquisse d'une histoire du bouddhisme fondée sur la critique archéologique des textes', *BEFEO*, XXXII, XXXIII, XXXIV, 1933–5.

Parmentier, H., 'L'architecture interpretée dans les bas-reliefs anciens de Java', *BEFEO*, VII, 1907.

Pigeaud, Th., *Java in the 14th century*, I-V, The Hague, 1960–3.

Pott, P.H., *Yoga and Yantra*, The Hague, 1966.

Permatilleke, L. and Silva, R., 'A Buddhist monastery type of ancient Ceylon showing Mahayanist influence', *Artibus Asiae*, XXX/1, 1968.

Raffles, T.S., *History of Java*, London, 1817.

Soekmono, *Candi, fungsi dan pengertiannya*, Jakarta, 1974.

_____, 'The archaeology of Central Java before 800 A.D.' (stencilled pamphlet), London, 1973.

Stohr, W. and Zoetmulder, P., *Les religions d'Indonésie*, Paris, 1968.

Stutterheim, T., *Tjandi Baraboedur, Naam, Virm en Beteekenis*, Batavia, 1929 (English translation: *Studies in Indonesian archeology*, The Hague, 1956).

Van Erp, T., *Barabudur, architectural description*, The Hague, 1931.

Van Leur, J.C., *Indonesian trade and society*, The Hague, 1955.

Van Lohuizen de Leew, J.E., 'South East Asian architecture and the stupa of Nandangarh', *Artibus Asiae*, XIX, 1956.

de Vink, J., *Report on an excavation on the east side of the Borobudur*, Leyden, 1912.

Vlekke, B.H.M., *Nusantara, A history of Indonesia*, The Hague, 1960.

Zimmer, H., *Kunstform und yoga in indischen Kultbild*, Berlin, 1926.

Chronological Table

| DATES A.D. | KINGS | | BOROBUDUR | BUILDINGS | EVENTS |
	SANJAYA	SAILENDRA			
?	Sanjaya				
732				The Cangal Inscription	
752 ?		Bhanu			
?		Visnu		Mendut I?	Sailendra raids in Indo-China
760 ?	Panongkaran				
775			Construction begun		
778				Kalasan I	
780 ?	Panunggalan			Sewu I	
782		Indra	Borobudur I	Kalasan II	
792			Borobudur II	Sewu II	
800 ?	Warak		Borobudur III	Kalasan III, Mendut II	
802				Sari	The Khmer king, Jayavarman II, frees himself from Javanese suzerainty
819	Garung	Samaratunga	Borobudur IV	Plaosan I	
824				Beginning of construction of Prambanan	Appearance of the double wall facing technique
832				Mendut III	
			Borobudur V	Plaosan II	
842	Pikatan			Prambanan	
856	Kayuwani			Asu	

Index

OXFORD IN ASIA PAPERBACKS

A delightful and informative library for readers
interested in China and South-East Asia, past and present

CAMBODIA
GEORGE COEDÈS
Angkor: An Introduction

CHINA
HAROLD ACTON
Peonies and Ponies
PETER FLEMING
Bayonets to Lhasa
PETER FLEMING
The Siege at Peking
W. SOMERSET MAUGHAM
On a Chinese Screen
OSBERT SITWELL
Escape with Me! An Oriental
  Sketch-book
AITCHEN WU
Turkistan Tumult
FRANCIS YOUNG HUSBAND
The Heart of a Continent

INDONESIA
S. TAKDIR ALISJAHBANA
Indonesia: Social and Cultural
  Revolution
VICKI BAUM
A Tale from Bali
MIGUEL COVARRUBIAS
Island of Bali
JACQUES DUMARCAY
Borobudur
JENNIFER LINDSAY
Javanese Gamelan
EDWIN M. LOEB
Sumatra: Its History and People
MOCHTAR LUBIS
Twilight in Djakarta
MADELON H. LULOFS
Coolie
ANNA MATHEWS
The Night of Purnama
COLIN McPHEE
A House in Bali
HICKMAN POWELL
The Last Paradise

BERYL DE ZOETE AND
WALTER SPIES
Dance and Drama in Bali
E. R. SCIDMORE
Java, Garden of the East
LADISLAO SZÉKELY
Tropic Fever: The Adventures of
  a Planter in Sumatra
EDWARD C. VAN NESS AND
SHITA PRAWIROHARDJO
Javanese Wayang Kulit
AUGUSTA DE WIT
Java: Facts and Fancies

MALAYSIA
ABDULLAH ABDUL KADIR
The Hikayat Abdullah
ISABELLA L. BIRD
The Golden Chersonese: Travels
  in Malaya in 1879
PIERRE BOULLE
Sacrilege in Malaya
C. C. BROWN (Editor)
Sejarah Melayu or Malay Annals
COLIN N. CRISSWELL
Rajah Charles Brooke: Monarch
  of All He Surveyed
K. M. ENDICOTT
An Analysis of Malay Magic
HENRI FAUCONNIER
The Soul of Malaya
W. R. GEDDES
Nine Dayak Nights
JOHN D. GIMLETTE
Malay Poisons and Charm Cures
JOHN D. GIMLETTE AND
H. W. THOMSON
A Dictionary of Malayan
  Medicine
A. G. GLENISTER
The Birds of the Malay Peninsula,
  Singapore and Penang
C. W. HARISSON
Illustrated Guide to the Federated
  Malay States (1923)

TOM HARRISSON
World Within
DENNIS HOLMAN
Noone of the Ulu
SYBIL KATHIGASU
No Dram of Mercy
JANET LIM
Sold for Silver
MALCOLM MacDONALD
Borneo People
AMBROSE B. RATHBORNE
Camping and Tramping in Malaya
J. T. THOMSON
Glimpses into Life in Malayan Land
RICHARD WINSTEDT
The Malay Magician

PHILIPPINES
AUSTIN COATES
Rizal

SINGAPORE
PATRICK ANDERSON
Snake Wine: A Singapore Episode
ROLAND BRADDELL
The Lights of Singapore
R. W. E. HARPER AND
HARRY MILLER
Singapore Mutiny
G. M. REITH
Handbook to Singapore (1907)
C. E. WURTZBURG
Raffles of the Eastern Isles

THAILAND
ERIK SEIDENFADEN
Guide to Bangkok
MALCOLM SMITH
A Physician at the Court of Siam
ERNEST YOUNG
The Kingdom of the Yellow Robe

YESTERDAY'S WORLD TODAY